ENDORSEMENTS

"Ruth Hendrickson is a stellar, seasoned, leader, and spiritual mother in the Body of Christ. Along with her committed personal journey with God, her years of experience have produced invaluable nuggets that will truly help any believer toward spiritual maturity. Her book, *Positioned,* is filled with treasures that will align and empower the reader to walk in their God-appointed destiny."

Dr. Patricia King
Founder of Patricia King Ministries
Founder of Women in Ministry Network

"Ruth is inviting you into an adventure with God where you will discover what it really means to live from your true identity, shift the way you see yourself, see God and the potential of your unique design. You will discover the lies that have held you back so you can courageously move ahead in your destiny with God.

"Where you have been doesn't define who you are, but it is an important part of your story. Ruth will help you discover who you are both naturally and spiritually so that you can design a life you can't wait to live!"

With anticipation,
Rob Stoppard
Destiny Unlimited International

"When I opened the pages of Ruth Hendrickson's new book titled: *Positioned: How To Be Aligned & Empowered To Walk In Your Divine Destiny*, I knew it would be amazing when I read the following words, '*It is time to sing your way to victory...It is time to burst forth in a victory song... a song with power to topple any mountain that stands in your way and dis-arm any enemy that stands against you.'*

"Amen! This book is amazing. It has revelation within every word and an impartation of faith as you read through each chapter. Ruth weaves personal life stories right alongside the Word. She invites you on a personal journey of limitless destiny with God as we all *'look a little higher.'* And the reason is…You were created for *MORE*."

Julie Meyer
IntoTheRiver.net – Julie's Online Worship Community
Singing the Scriptures TV Show
Singing through the Psalms

"Most books on fulfilling your spiritual destiny only inspire you. This book goes far beyond that. Drawing on her many years of experience working in emotional healing, Ruth Hendrickson provides powerful and rich insights in the ways we can move past the internal barriers that keep us from fulfilling our God-given destiny. This book will do more than inform you. It will empower you!"

Dr. J. Scott McDermott
Lead Pastor
Washington Crossing UMC

POSITIONED

HOW TO BE ALIGNED
& EMPOWERED TO WALK
IN YOUR DIVINE DESTINY

RUTH
HENDRICKSON

LIFEWISE BOOKS

POSITIONED

HOW TO BE ALIGNED AND EMPOWERED TO WALK IN YOUR DIVINE DESTINY

BY RUTH HENDRICKSON

Published by:

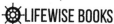 LIFEWISE BOOKS

PO BOX 1072
Pinehurst, TX 77362
LifeWiseBooks.com

Cover Design and Interior Layout | Yvonne Parks | PearCreative.ca

To contact the author | www.RuthHendrickson.org

ISBN (Print): 978-1-947279-59-9
ISBN (Ebook): 978-1-947279-60-5

SPECIAL ACKNOWLEDGEMENT

A huge thank you to my husband Mark and my children, Eleya, Steven, Marissa, Donna and Alan. We journey through life together holding onto God!

TABLE OF CONTENTS

Foreword by Sandie Freed   9

Introduction   11

Chapter 1 | Head Space   15

Chapter 2 | Who Am I?   35

Chapter 3 | The Making of a Wardrobe   51

Chapter 4 | Dangerous Caverns   71

Chapter 5 | Unlocking the Ball and Chain   85

Chapter 6 | Graveyard to Garden   103

Chapter 7 | Roaring Lions   119

Chapter 8 | Moments and Mountain Moving   139

Conclusion   153

About the Author   161

Endnotes   163

Bibles Cited   175

Works Cited   177

FOREWORD

I have known Ruth Hendrickson for many years. When she speaks, there is a tangible anointing that leads people towards pathways of freedom. Ruth is a gifted counselor and deliverance minister. I continue to be amazed at how God has given her so many keys to set the captives free. She is a treasure to the Body of Christ.

In her timely book, *Positioned; to Be Aligned and Empowered to Walk in Your Divine Destiny*, Ruth writes, "God is asking 'Do you see what I see?' Everything changes when we see through God's lens or perspective rather than our own."

God loves to restore our potential and purpose. Throughout Scripture we find many who seemed hopeless, helpless and fearful, however, God saw their potential. Remember Gideon? He saw himself as the least in his tribe, but God saw a mighty warrior! Throughout the book we are reminded that God will meet us right where we are at and invite us to go further than we ever dreamed we could go.

I love how Ruth focuses on how the Father (God) sees us. God does not focus on our flaws or our mistakes. Rather the Father sees us completed in Jesus. Ruth's book is laced with this question from the Father, "Do you see what I see?" As I read this question, I found myself stopping to ask if I was seeing myself as the Father sees me.

Another statement that caught my attention is "Every failure that we encounter throughout our lives is an opportunity to grow into the person that God has called us to be." To me this means there is really no failure at all. Rather, it's an opportunity to better ourselves by God's grace. Through the book, Ruth walks us through Scripture, invites us into aspects of her personal life, and helps us to see how God intentionally positions us to fully walk into our divine destiny.

Remember, the bottom line is we all need to know God and know who we are in Him.

I pray that as you journey through this book with Ruth that you will be amazed at how God ministers to the very core of your being and that you will move forward with renewed hope and freedom!

Sandie Freed
Sandie Freed Ministries

INTRODUCTION

God is raising up a mighty army consisting of His healed and whole children. Some of you have been in very difficult places and feel like you are being squeezed beyond what you can bear. I hear the Lord saying, "Release your frustration!" What feels like it is crushing you cannot actually destroy you. He is using that crushing to refine you. On the other side is joy and freedom like you have never known.

There is ground being taken. In places where the lies have been tightly adhered I see a bottle of Holy Spirit Goo-Gone. There is no scrubbing required. As Holy Spirit pours the liquid over the lies, the truth automatically replaces the lie. As I have been typing, there are times when I highlight something and replace it with something else. That is the picture. The Holy Spirit highlights, washes the area, and replaces it with His label. You are being shined and polished to more fully reflect the glory of God.

For some of you, dreams have been crushed and you feel like you have missed your opportunity to walk into your destiny. I hear the Holy Spirit saying that the only thing that has held you back is fear. It is time to put one foot in front of the other and move forward.

Stagnant water begins to stink. He is calling you to swim in the River of Life. As that river washes over you, the stench will be washed away. It is not too late. The dreams that He planted within you can still bear fruit, and not just a little fruit, but much fruit. Allow yourself to dream with Him. He will direct your steps. But you must choose to take the first step.

For those of you who have had demonic assignments against you, it is time to sing your way to victory. You have stood, declared, and fought and yet felt like there was no victory. There is victory. It is time to burst forth in a victory song. Allow yourself to align with the armies of Heaven. They will lead the way when you provide the song. Allow the song to well up from deep inside. God has placed it there. It is a song with enough power to topple any mountain that stands in your way and disarm any enemy that stands against you.

Hopeless—for those who have been sitting in a pool of hopelessness. I hear the Lord asking, "Do you really want to be healed?" Now is the time. I call forth the well of joy and speak life to your weary bones. You will sing, dance and rejoice in God your Father. All is not lost. You were designed with a purpose. Get up; get dressed and look for the goodness of God. It is available wherever you are right now.

I pray that you will experience an ever-increasing measure of the love and freedom that the Lord has for you. You are positioned to take ground. No more standing back. It is time to advance. Listen to Him. He has the next step all mapped out. Trust Him.

So, find a comfortable spot, (grab a coffee, tea, or water) and join me on a journey. This journey will speak truth and bring freedom. This journey will draw you close to the heartbeat of God and position you to be aligned and empowered to walk into your divine destiny.

"Lord, You know everything there is to know about me.
You perceive every movement of my heart and soul,
and You understand my every thought before it even enters my mind.
You are so intimately aware of me, Lord.
You read my heart like an open book
and You know all the words I'm about to speak
before I even start a sentence!
You know every step I will take before my journey even begins.
You've gone into my future to prepare the way,
and in kindness You follow behind me
to spare me from the harm of my past.
With Your hand of love upon my life,
You impart a blessing to me.
This is just too wonderful, deep, and incomprehensible!
Your understanding of me brings me wonder and strength."

PSALM 139:1-6 TPT

CHAPTER ONE

HEAD SPACE

"Christians who live out of who they really are cannot be crippled by the opinions of others. They no longer work to fit into other people's expectations; they burn with the realization of who the Father says they are." [1]
BILL JOHNSON

THEORIES, LAWS AND BELIEF SYSTEMS

Jayden was a rambunctious little boy with a spirit of adventure. Like the best actor, he would don his Superman cape, stand up tall, flex his muscles and become Superman, running around the house with his cape flying in the wind behind him. His little face was full of determination as he conquered every foe in his imagination. With each step, his mind entered further into the realm of Superman until he firmly believed that he could fly and land wherever he wanted! Flying past the window, he sees his sister outside. Superman to the rescue! Running as hard and fast as his little feet would carry him, he heads straight for her without a thought about the plate glass window that stood between them. As Jayden hits the glass, it shatters. Shards of glass flew everywhere, including into his little body. Jayden found his kryptonite and learned the theory of gravity at the same time.

Step back for a moment and remember yourself as a young child. Without realizing it, you probably believed you were invincible. Children are naturally curious beyond measure. A child will touch anything and explore any place. They see the world as a challenge to be conquered and believe they can conquer it. Children are convinced that the entire world revolves around them.

We see the wonder and excitement in their eyes and sometimes wish that we could see life the way they do. A child's eyes have not experienced life as we have so their vision is not blurred nor is their belief system scarred. They see with clarity and wonder as they watch a butterfly break out of its cocoon, touch a flower, pick up insects, learn to skip rocks in a pond and watch the ripples form in the water. It is no wonder that we are told in Scripture to become like little children.[2]

Our hearts break as we see them experience the bumps and bruises of life. We hold them and comfort them as they experience the painful side. Often, we cry with them as they shed the tears that come with the cuts and scrapes, bumps and bruises of life. We try to help them process the pain when others call them names, when they fail, or when their dreams are crushed.

All the while there is a belief system developing deep within the child. These beliefs are either good, life-giving, and precious, which will take them far and instill a healthy identity of worth and value; or the beliefs are unhealthy, potentially holding the child back from the dreams that God has placed deep within them. When fully realized, unhealthy belief systems often lead to issues such as fear, insecurity and lack of identity and worth. Each one of us has a foundation of theories and laws that we operate from, our own belief system: a collection of cultural experiences, life experiences, teachings and modeling from which we unknowingly develop our individual beliefs and behavior patterns. It is from this platform that we live and view life.

Whether we realize it or not, God is always asking us a question. *Do you see what I see?* He is actually asking us this question from the day we are born until the day we die. His desire is always to draw us closer to Him. He longs to teach us, to equip us, and most of all, to have a vibrant life-giving relationship with us. There is always an open invitation to see things with greater clarity and often differently than we have in the past.

HOW DO WE LEARN TO SEE WHAT HE SEES?

First, we take a good look at the theories, laws and belief systems that we have developed over the years. We stop blaming others for our bumps and bruises, and we ask God to bring healing to those places where pain has clouded our vision. Ultimately, we align our vision with God's vision of us, our circumstances, and our future.

ARE YOU READY?
GOD DESIRES TO UNLOCK GREATNESS IN YOUR LIFE.

He fashioned and positioned you before you were even born to go beyond your fears, insecurities, bumps, bruises and hurts. The Psalmist reminds us He has given you every tool that you need to be free from beliefs that would hold you back.

"You formed my innermost being, shaping my delicate inside and my intricate outside, and wove them all together in my mother's womb. I thank You, God, for making me so mysteriously complex! Everything You do is marvelously breathtaking. It simply amazes me to think about it! How thoroughly You know me, Lord! You even formed every bone in my body when You created me in the secret place, carefully, skillfully shaping me from nothing to something. You saw who You created me to be before I became me! Before I'd ever see the light of day, the number of days You planned for me were already recorded in Your book." [3]

He has created you for more. He has created me for more. Our potential is limitless with God. No matter where you are at right now, I can tell you that you were designed by God to be a person of impact! Can you see yourself through the eyes of the heavenly Father?

POWERFUL PERCEPTIONS

Perceptions impact our belief system and become more ingrained than we realize. We all want to be loved and accepted. Every culture, people group, and generation has collective perceptions. We take these perceptions, compare ourselves and develop our personal reality.

In 1959, Mattel introduced the first Barbie doll. She quickly became every young girl's perception of a perfect woman's body. While I don't consciously remember Barbie impacting my own self-perception or my belief system, I must admit that somewhere along the line I determined that my body was not correctly proportioned. In addition to my negative body image, I also struggled in math and had a speech impediment. Unbeknownst to me, all this was feeding a negative belief system which was attaching to my core identity and further blurring my ability to "see what He sees."

We all have our own personalized list of things we believe are wrong with us. Often this is internalized and never verbalized. In fact, it goes into a land known as denial. No matter how much we try to hide it, explain it, or run from it, inevitably we will be found by it.

Here's a fact for the men: Do you know that the sought after chiseled body and the six-pack abs that you work tirelessly at the gym to attain would have been considered overweight just a few generations ago? I recently asked a youth pastor, "What image issues do guys struggle with?"

He explained that young men are asking themselves two questions, "Am I sexy enough?" and, "Do girls find me attractive?" If the girls are not interested, this perception often leads a young man to a negative body image. And this is only a precursor to college, where one study states that 95% of college students are dissatisfied with their bodies.[4] Needless to say, issues with body image are not relegated only to youth and college students; many people continue to struggle throughout their adult lives.

Up to now, I have primarily used examples of body image. However, what we *see* reflects in all areas of our lives. 1 Corinthians describes this lens perfectly and gives us a promise.

> *"Now we see things imperfectly, like puzzling reflections in a mirror, but then we will see everything with perfect clarity. All that I know now is partial and incomplete, but then I will know everything completely, just as God now knows me completely."* [5]

Take note that Paul says we see imperfectly. This tells us that not all our beliefs and perceptions about self, life, or others are necessarily clear, focused or correct. However, we need to pay attention to the words *but then,* as this means that something follows, which is very important. What follows may be the very thing that gives us hope. If we don't move past the negative, we will never see the promised positive. We are told that we will see everything with perfect clarity. There is a measure of great and godly clarity that can be experienced on earth. In other words, we are promised that we can and will see what He sees.

Another Scripture that speaks to this says it this way, *"How could you say to your friend, 'Let me show you where you're wrong,' when you're guilty of even more"?* [6] This verse tells me that my own vision and belief system needs to be in the process of being cleaned up and corrected before I can truly help others.

For me personally, the internalized list that I developed eventually created a lens through which I processed and experienced life. It had developed, unknowingly, at the time of my conception and continued to form as the years amassed. Although I may not bear the full blame for my belief system, I am the only one who is responsible for it. No one can tell me what to think or what to believe. Even if it happened while I was too young to understand, God has created me to reach a point where I must assume responsibility. Not only that, but when I reach that point He is also willing to provide the tools that I need to realign with His will. In other words, if I allow Him to, He will correct my vision so I can see how He sees.

Whenever our focus is not aligned with God's focus and our beliefs are not aligned with His beliefs, confusion will reign. Scripture states, *"For God is not a God of disorder but of peace..."* [7] Where there is a lack of peace, we can be assured that the fullness of God is not present. It never ceases to amaze me that the God of the universe wants a relationship with us, you and me. He longs to share His dreams with us and He longs for us to see the world through His eyes. Our God is a God of peace, so not only does our vision change, but we also learn to walk in a level of peace that can only come from Him.

> God is asking, "Do you see what I see?" Everything changes when we see through God's lens or perspective rather than our own.

Look again at the Corinthians passage above. Paul states that there *will* come a day when we *will* see everything clearly. The funny thing is that when Scripture uses the word *will*, it means *will*. God is faithful to His promises and there is no hidden meaning to the word *will*. In fact, that word should jump off the page and give us hope because our God is so incredibly faithful. Paul recognizes this and more as he prays for the Ephesian church.

> *"...asking God, the glorious Father of our Lord Jesus Christ, to give you spiritual wisdom and insight so that you might grow in your knowledge of God. I pray that your hearts will be flooded with light so that you can understand the confident hope He has given to those He called-His holy people who are His rich and glorious inheritance."* [8]

When Scripture uses the term *heart* (I pray that your heart will be flooded), it is not referring to the muscle that pumps blood through our bodies. Rather it is referring to *"the center of our physical and spiritual being, combining our intellectual understanding and our personal affections. So, Paul prays that the 'eyes of [their] heart(s)' will be enlightened by God to love the things that God loves, so that these Christians will see the world the way God does, which is the way it really is."* [9] Therefore, we can be assured that as we walk with the Lord, our vision will become clear and confusion will flee.

I want you to notice that this passage says that we are called "*His holy people who are His rich and glorious inheritance.*"[10] So, what does it mean to be God's inheritance? When I think of inheritance, I think in practical terms, namely financial and material provision. It is not something that I earn, but something that is left to me upon someone else's death. When someone dies, we often talk about their legacy because it is also a form of inheritance. Legacy is the impact that another person has on me, that I intentionally carry forward in my life, impacting others.

Jesus Christ died on the cross so we could receive our full inheritance. Our heavenly Father faithfully and steadily invests in our healing, deliverance, identity and destiny. You could say He has a stake in our past, present, and future. Every move He makes is with us in mind, and for the legacy He has fashioned for us.

Here are a few questions to consider as you continue this journey toward seeing as He sees.

1. What will change if I fully realize what God declares, that I am one of His holy people?

2. What will change if I realize that I truly am God's inheritance?

3. How does that impact how I see myself?

COMPOUND INTEREST

When we invest money, our goal is to make money. When the initial money makes more money (interest), and the interest begins to make money, that is called compounding interest.

God never designed us to live in isolation. He is the one who created the concepts of family, community, and relationship. One of the many functions of the family unit is to model a relationship with the heavenly Father. As this relationship is modeled, it impacts our belief system. For example, if you had a loving earthly father, you will likely have a positive view of Father God. If you were abused by your father, you may view God as being judgmental, harsh, or unloving. I don't want to pick on the guys, so let me bring some balance in by specifically stating that our mothers play a huge role in our image of God, also.

To summarize, the healthier the parental figures are in our lives, the more comfortable we will be in our family, community, and relationships. God's intention was and is that our family units would model His love for us and the body of Christ would model His love for His bride. You could say that what is modeled actually becomes compounded interest in our lives as it impacts who we are and how we view God.

I remember standing at the kitchen door watching my husband and youngest son walking in our back yard. I noticed that they were walking the same way. The thing that strikes me now, when thinking about that moment, is that we are called to walk the same way as our heavenly Father. My son was never *taught* to walk like his father, instead it came out in the very essence of who he is. When we walk with the Lord, our relationship grows like compounding interest, or genetic inheritance, until we inevitably begin to walk like Him, talk like Him, and think like Him.

In Acts, we meet a young man by the name of Stephen. Stephen walked with the Lord and loved the Lord so much that he offended the wrong people. In the book of Acts, much as it is today, many people desired to silence those who were telling others about Jesus, so Stephen's stance was unpopular. However, I believe that Stephen's statement at the end of his life set the stage to radically change both the belief system and the worldview of at least one individual.

> *"The Jewish leaders were infuriated by Stephen's accusation, and they shook their fists at him in rage. But Stephen, full of the Holy Spirit, gazed steadily into heaven and saw the glory of God, Jesus standing in the place of honor at God's right hand. And he told them: 'Look, I see the heavens opened and the Son of Man standing in the place of honor at God's right hand!' Then they put their hands over their ears and began shouting. They rushed at him and dragged him out of the city and began to stone him. His accusers took off their coats and laid them at the feet of a young man named Saul. As they stoned him, Stephen prayed, 'Lord Jesus, receive my spirit.' He fell to his knees, shouting, 'Lord, don't charge them with this sin!' And with that, he died."[11]*

Stephen walked so closely with the Lord that amid his pain, he looked up and saw the very throne room of heaven. In other words, as God was asking, *Do you see what I see?* Stephen could confidently answer, *"YES!"* Stephen had walked with the Lord long enough and closely enough to know and trust the faithfulness of God. In other words, the investment that Stephen put into that relationship had compounded interest. When faced with not only a challenging moment, but his own death, Stephen drew from that account, leaned into his Savior and gazed into Heaven. Stephen saw the royal throne of his Father and, quite incredibly, cried out for forgiveness for his murderers. In the center of this stage was a young man named Saul, carefully watching these events unfold. I believe that this scene seared into Saul's memory.

Stephen was able to declare that his vision was aligned with God's vision. In his death, a legacy was passed from Stephen to a very unsuspecting Saul who was also being positioned for alignment with his destiny in a way he never saw coming.

MASSIVE OVERHAUL

As Saul continued to mature and develop his personal belief system, his hatred for those following Jesus also grew. He became a dedicated and feared persecutor of believers like Stephen. Those who had a dedication and love for the Lord were not strangers to the name of *Saul* because they understood that his presence ultimately meant their imprisonment or even death. However, as the old saying goes, that applecart was about to be upset.

You may be familiar with Saul's Damascus Road experience (Acts 9) as God met him, blinded him, and set him on a new course. His life was redirected by the power of God.

"Meanwhile, Saul was uttering threats with every breath and was eager to kill the Lord's followers. So, he went to the high priest. He requested letters addressed to the synagogues in Damascus, asking for their cooperation in the arrest of any followers of the Way he found there. He wanted to bring them—both men and women—back to Jerusalem in chains.

"As he was approaching Damascus on this mission, a light from heaven suddenly shone down around him. He fell to the ground and heard a voice saying to him, 'Saul! Saul! Why are you persecuting me?' 'Who are you, Lord?' Saul asked. And the voice replied, 'I am Jesus, the One you are persecuting! Now get up and go into the city, and you will be told what you must do.' The men with Saul stood speechless, for they heard the sound of someone's voice but saw no one! Saul picked himself up off the ground, but

when he opened his eyes he was blind. So, his companions led him by hand to Damascus. He remained there blind for three days and did not eat or drink." [12]

In the last section, we asked a question, *Do you see what I see?* Note that God literally blinded Saul. This man, who was so sure of himself, had to be led around. Why? Because God was radically adjusting his focus! When Ananias arrived, God restored much more than Saul's physical sight, He turned his belief system upside down!

"So Ananias went and found Saul. He laid his hands on him and said, 'Brother Saul, the Lord Jesus, who appeared to you on the road, has sent me so that you might regain your sight and be filled with the Holy Spirit.' Instantly something like scales fell from Saul's eyes, and he regained his sight. Then he got up and was baptized. Afterward he ate some food and regained his strength." [13]

In Scripture, we find Saul was also referred to as Paul. Saul was his Roman name while Paul was a name that was familiar to the Gentiles. We will learn that Saul's primary sphere of influence and ministry would ultimately be to the Gentiles therefore we will see the name Paul used frequently in the Bible. In Philippians 3, we see Paul giving his pedigree and his rationale for his past behavior. Paul states,

"I was circumcised when I was eight days old. I am a pure-blooded citizen of Israel and a member of the tribe of Benjamin—a real Hebrew if there ever was one! I was a member of the Pharisees, who demand the strictest obedience to the Jewish law. I was so zealous that I harshly persecuted the church. And as for righteousness, I obeyed the law without fault." [14] Paul goes on to describe how radically his belief system was

changed, how much he loves the Lord, and ultimately, he states that he knows his destiny: "...but I focus on one thing: Forgetting the past and looking forward to what lies ahead, I press on to reach the end of the race and receive the heavenly prize for which God, through Christ Jesus, is calling us." [15]

Paul was not ashamed to share where he came from, but he also knew that it didn't impact where he was going either. He walked with a radically refocused vision and belief system. Paul could state with assurance that he was beloved of God and was walking in God's intended purpose and destiny on this earth with an ultimate destiny of heaven.

I like the story of Saul because God met him in a powerful way. Although Scripture doesn't explicitly state that Saul wrestled with God as his belief system was changed, I imagine he did to some degree. After all, Saul was human just like us. I'm sure he had questions, but he was an excellent student and learned that God is a great conversationalist.

Are there ways in our lives that God is positioning us to move into unknown and unchartered territory? Be aware, that much like Saul, these may be areas to which we were once in opposition.

RIPPLES OF IMPACT

It has always interested me that most of the Pharisees, the religious leaders of that day, missed the Messiah. When you throw a rock in a body of water, there are ripples that continue for a considerable distance. That miss by the Pharisees of Jesus' day still ripples through and impacts the culture of today. Many are still looking for the Messiah and believe that Jesus was just a person or maybe a prophet, but not the promised Messiah. I would venture to say that many men and women who were designed to impact the Kingdom for Jesus have missed their destiny call.

Don't get me wrong. It's not just the religious leaders of then and now. We are all guilty of missing the invitation of God at some point. Pride is a huge stumbling block for all of humanity. Many have missed God's ripple effect since Jesus birth and death.

Burger King had a slogan for years, "Have it Your Way," and we all know the famous Nike slogan, "Just Do It." The Baby Boomers were traditionally called the Me Generation and, interestingly enough. some are applying Generation Me to the Millennials.[16] From the very beginning, with Adam and Eve choosing to eat the forbidden fruit, and continuing on through today, humanity has always struggled to fully align with God and walk into its intended destiny.

Years ago, I was attending a conference in Toronto, Canada. The altar call was for those who had been ignoring their call to ministry. I folded my arms across my chest and sat there like a stone! Later that night, God and I had a very long conversation as I wrestled with what He was asking me to do. After all, I did not have a seminary degree, nor did I want one. I didn't see myself as educated enough, gifted enough or valuable enough to be in ministry. I had five young children at home, and I was 100% sure that my husband would never be on board with what God was asking of me. In addition, I had a million reasons why this wasn't a good idea. However, God had a different viewpoint.

As God spoke to my heart, He began to shift my focus and asked me to radically walk with Him. I wonder what went through Saul's mind as he waited for Ananias to arrive. I know that I had many questions as I began to move forward into a new season with shaky steps and battle my belief system as God began redefining me. I came home from that conference to discover that God had had a conversation with my husband also. What I believed Mark would never be on board with, was already a done deal.

A few years later, I found myself on pastoral staff at a local church. In my mind, it was a three to five-year position. However, as the years went on, I had to realign myself with God's viewpoint and His game plan. It would be over thirteen years before I left that position. God put me in that situation to equip and train me for the next stage/season of my life. He will do the same for you. We all need to remember that we are on a journey through life with Him.

> He is faithful to use both the steps and missteps
> in our journey if our focus is on Him.

I want to encourage you to never stop short of all that God has for you. Yes, there are twists and turns along the way, but God is faithful. Keep the focus on Him and you'll be okay.

I told you the story of my trip to Toronto and working through a call into ministry. As God and I wrestled through the night, I asked that I would be able to raise my children first. As the years went by, I would sometimes feel stuck and wonder if I had made a misstep. I eventually realized that I had to close the door to that question. Keeping that door open posed a potential risk to my walk into my destiny because it could open a door to regret. I repeatedly surrendered to God. On this side, I can see that He used that season for training and equipping me for what I am walking in now. He was moving deeper and further than I could see in the moment. The question was not if I had made a misstep, the question was if I was willing to radically follow Him and move one step at a time.

With that said, I want you to understand something. My belief system didn't shift overnight. It was a battle that was at times fought moment by moment. God was and still is more interested in my heart and my belief system than I am.

Over the years, God brought people into my life who would speak the very heartbeat of God's plans into me. These people didn't necessarily know me or the dreams that were within me. You could say that they were God's mouthpiece, truly modern-day prophets. Some were well-known and operated in national and international circles while others were only really known by God. The key was that God sent the same underlying message to my heart over and over.

The best way I can describe it is that He was adding His fertilizer on those words that He had planted deep within me during our conversation in Toronto. And, as He was fertilizing my hopes and dreams, He was also adjusting the lens on my belief system. Beliefs such as "I'm not good enough" or "I'm not educated enough" had to come down. I had to go through a shift; the lens through which I saw myself and viewed life had to fundamentally change if I was to step into the calling that God had on my life.

As followers of Jesus, we are often quick to quote Scripture about God's faithfulness and to use quotes such as "those He calls, He also equips." While those quotes are good and true, we tend to forget that there is a very real battle for the mind. We must give people space to process through their fears and insecurities. We must give God access to the very areas that do not align with His plans in order to bring healing. We must work through our own issues. And, at the same time, He will patiently strengthen other areas that need to mature as we journey with Him.

I still battle doubts and fears. I have resolved that the rest of the journey will include continual refocusing and redefining. However, with each adjustment of the lens, the journey becomes clearer. Day by day and moment by moment, my belief system aligns better with my Lord's. The path I am traveling becomes more evident as I journey hand in hand with Him. Like Paul, I can forget the past and focus on what is ahead. And what a glorious journey it is!

SPIRITUAL MUSCLE BUILDING

This section is intended to help you dive deeper into your own life. While I may pose the questions, I also understand that some people are not comfortable with hearing the voice of God. That's okay! Don't stop; do not give up and do not run from this. As we ask the Lord about the questions below, sit back and listen. Then write what comes to mind. You don't need to strive over it. Just lean into the arms of our wonderful heavenly Father. Trust God. As you journey through this book, you will get more comfortable. So be sure to come back later and ask the questions again. You'll be surprised at your growth as you go through this process, step by step.

QUESTIONS

1. Ask the Holy Spirit to reveal the most significant battle that you face within your belief system.

2. What is the area of your belief system that you feel most insecure in? Does it align with God's Word? Why, or why not?

ACTION STEPS

1. Set aside some time to spend with the Lord. Confess the area(s) of your belief system that doesn't align with His heart and His Word.

2. Then take time to listen. Remember, our God is a great conversationalist. He may give you a picture, a word, or a Scripture. Allow Him to speak. Record what you see, sense or hear.

PRAYER AND DECLARATION

Heavenly Father, I release to you the areas of my belief system that do not align with Your Word. Your Word states that I will know the truth and the truth will set me free. Therefore, I declare that I will know and comprehend Your Word and that I will increasingly walk in truth and freedom. Your Word also states that Scripture is God-breathed and useful to teach us what is true.

Therefore, I make a commitment that I will spend time in Your Word, hear and receive the truth that is contained in Your Word. And since Your Word states that it is one of the tools that You use to prepare us to walk in the fullness of relationship with You, I declare that I will walk with You and You will teach me to do all You have called me to do. I declare that I am Your beloved son/daughter and that I will live in the truth from the very Kingdom of Heaven.

SCRIPTURAL BASIS:

John 8:32, 2 Timothy 3:16-17

CHAPTER TWO
WHO AM I?

"Don't waste your time consuming what makes you weak. Spend your time pressing in for the Presence. Become so intimate with Jesus, so full of Him, that it does not matter what challenges in life present themselves to you. You will be so spiritually full that you can feed a multitude of other people's needs. Jesus will give you more than enough."[1]

HEIDI BAKER

IDEN'TITY, *noun* Sameness, as distinguished from similitude and diversity. We speak of the *identity* of goods found, the *identity* of persons, or of personal *identity.*[2]

Ruth's Version: Identity is what makes you uniquely you and me uniquely me. However, for the follower of Jesus Christ, it is much more. What is so amazing is that God desires to define our identity in alignment with His view of us. So, let the journey begin!

WHO AM I?

What are the roles that try to shape my identity? For example, I am a daughter, a wife, a mother, a pastor, a teacher, a speaker, and a follower of Jesus, just to name a few. On the surface, these all sound very positive. However, the whole issue of identity goes much deeper than the roles we play in life.

For example, I was not the perfect daughter. I was strong-willed (still am), stubborn (still am), I did things behind my parents back (didn't we all), and periodically got myself and my friends in trouble. In other words, I wasn't perfect. But my parents still claim me as their daughter and being a daughter is part of my identity.

I am also a parent. I did the best I knew how in raising my children. However, don't tell them they were raised by an imperfect mother! Even with my imperfections, a mother is still part of my identity.

When I was very young, I had a severe speech impediment. As you read this, please remember I grew up in the 1960's, and the language wasn't politically correct! As school was looming closer and closer, the suggestion was made that I may be retarded (remember, I said this was before PC days). At some point, my parents took me to be evaluated and it was determined that I was not retarded but should start school early. And so I began kindergarten at the age of four. As I struggled to be understood, there was an open door to be labeled as retarded, or in current vernacular, intellectually disabled.[3]

What it boils down to is that many people get stuck with their failures, and failure ultimately becomes their identity. The identities that revolve around failure usually go deep underground and are heavily wrapped in shame. As we try to mask a real or perceived failure, it becomes easy to identify from a positional identity. In fact, when you ask most people who they are, their response will usually be what they do. I am a CEO of XYZ Company; I am a pastor or I am "just a mom." You can fill in the blanks with your own usual response without even thinking about it. Although positional identity is part of your story, it is not the fullness of your story. To really talk about identity, we must make a shift how we view both real and perceived failure and shortcomings.

> Every failure that we encounter throughout life is an opportunity to grow into the person that God has called us to be.

The questions become: Who defines my identity? Do I allow my failure(s) to identify who I am? Do I allow the labels (retarded) to define who I am? Or do I ultimately allow God to define me?

These are very serious questions. However, let me caution you, they do not require inward navel-gazing, but they do require upward God-gazing. Remember, God is asking "Do you see what I see?" How we answer that question is vital to our journey. As we ask God for revelation, we also must listen and prepare to act on what He is showing us.

I do not doubt that David struggled with this. David was a young man in the Old Testament. I always appreciated it when my kids did their chores, and that is precisely what David was doing when we meet him. As the youngest, his job was to tend the sheep. However, as he was out with the sheep, the prophet appeared at his father's door.[4] You must understand that this wasn't just any prophet, but this was Samuel, THE PROPHET of God! This knowledge would have certainly sent the family scurrying to give him a proper welcome.

Samuel was on assignment to anoint the next king of Israel. He asked to see all Jesse's children. As they passed by this mighty man of God one by one, I am sure the brothers' knees were knocking, no matter how tough they thought they were. Samuel had his ear turned to the heavens and, much to Samuel's shock, no one who passed by was God's chosen one. Since Samuel was on assignment from God, he knew he had to find the correct child. Therefore, Samuel had to ask about any other children.

Step back for a moment and put yourself in David's shoes. Imagine David suddenly being called in from the field. Did David wonder why he wasn't called in with everyone else? Did rejection have an opportunity to take root? Is it possible that he felt he was not as highly valued as his siblings? Scripture doesn't tell us what David felt as he realized he was the focus of Samuel's visit.

We do know that David was an actual person with feelings just like us. Again, the prophet's visit was huge! Realizing that all his brothers had passed by or spent time with the prophet would have left him wondering what he had missed. David was the youngest, the least and the forgotten child at this event. Yet, suddenly, Samuel was anointing him as the next king of Israel.

In moments like these, there is the potential for our God-given identity to get lost. My identity could have quickly become *retarded, stupid,* or *worthless.* The same situation existed with David's identity. He could have become the *youngest, unimportant, forgotten, invisible* or *not worthy.* Any of these carry the potential to feed a developing unhealthy and ungodly belief system rather than developing a radical dependence on God.

Thankfully, identity doesn't have to be lost. In fact, God intends that we find our identity in Him. Scripture explicitly states that we were created in the image of God.[5] Each of us was carefully planned. Not one of us was an accident.

> *"I knew you before I formed you in your mother's womb. Before you were born, I set you apart and appointed you as my prophet to the nations."* [6]

Before reading any further, read that verse over again and substitute by stating where God has you in this season of your life. For example, *I knew you, Ruth, before I formed you in your mother's womb. Ruth, I knew you before you were even born, I set you apart and appointed you as a mother/father to your children (as an equipper of the saints, as a CEO for XYZ company etc).* Take a moment and thank God for His goodness!

Wherever we are, in whatever season of life, what we do is only part of what defines us. Ultimately, we are defined by so much more! Why do we hide the *real me*? Great question! We all unintentionally or intentionally hide behind masks. So, let's take a look at the making of a mask.

MASK-MAKING 101

Masks can be simple or elaborate. I cannot think of a child who doesn't like to dress up. My mother would make costumes for my daughters and the neighbors' girls so they could perform their favorite musical in our basement. The boys would dress up as mighty hunters ready to capture the unsuspecting animal for dinner. Boys and girls alike dress up as their favorite superhero, destined to save the world! They dream of leaping over grand buildings in a single bound and killing the wild beast. In fact, this is mentioned in Scripture.

"In your strength I can crush an army; with my God I can scale any wall." [7]

Children inherently know they are created to do great, mighty, amazing, and creative exploits! Growing up, I was expected to be the perfect preacher's kid. Of course, I found ways to rebel, just to the line, so I usually wouldn't get in trouble. However, in the midst of that, I also learned to wear a mask. If there were problems at home, I didn't share. If I was hurting, I didn't share. And of course, at school I was the *untouchable* preacher's kid. Sure, I survived. But I also learned to wear a mask. We all learn to wear a mask of some form.

What mask did you wear growing up? How did that mask impact your life?

Remember that forgotten young boy who was out tending the sheep and almost missed the prophet? Well, he was indeed the one that Samuel was looking for. Oddly enough, Samuel anointed David as king, left and went back home. What did David do? He went back to tending sheep.

What is the message in this scene? Sometimes the identity to which God has called us, is something we must grow into!

As we step back into David's life, we find Jesse (his father) sending him to the battlefront to take food to his brothers. All his brothers were part of King Saul's army. As David comes on the scene, he finds the mighty Israelite army quaking in fear. Even King Saul, who was a seasoned warrior, is holding back rather than leading his men into victory. Why? We know that the Spirit of the Lord had departed from Saul and the Lord's strength was definitely needed for this battle, not man's. As God's people, they should have been full of God-given confidence and able to fearlessly walk into battle against the giant. Since their faith and focus were not secure, the door was open for the Philistine to control the Israelites. Whenever we are not walking in our identity, we open the door to be taken captive by something or someone else.

As David begins to ask questions, he is reminded of his place. Basically, he was told to stay in his own lane. By the world's viewpoint, not to mention his brother's viewpoint, David was too young to be of any value and they were not afraid to remind him of that. However, God had a different plan.

Even as a boy, David had a heart that sought after God. We know that he was a worshipper; so, I imagine that even as he tended sheep, he was worshipping the living God. While the Israelites were quaking in fear, David asked a telling question, *"What will be done for the man who kills this Philistine and removes this disgrace from Israel?"*[8] David was seeing past the present reality into the heavenly realm to God's intended purpose. Still, the temptation came to put on a mask.

> Often, at the juncture of destiny, there comes a temptation to put on something that God didn't intend for us to wear. While new armor may be required for the new season, it must still be the armor that is designed for us, not for someone else.

When I train ministry teams, it is not unusual for them to try to mimic my ministry style. While this is okay during the training process, they must also reach a point where they are taking the tools that I am providing and combining them with their own personal giftedness. God didn't create duplicate models, He created unique individuals.

> *"'Don't worry about this Philistine,' David told Saul, 'I'll go fight him!' 'Don't be ridiculous,' Saul replied. 'There's no way you can fight this Philistine and possibly win! You're only a boy, and he's been a man of war since his youth.' But David persisted, 'I have been taking care of my father's sheep and goats,' he said. 'When a lion or a bear comes to steal a lamb from the flock, I go after it with a club and rescue the lamb from its mouth. If the animal turns on me, I catch it by the jaw and club it to death. I have done this to both lions and bears, and I'll do it to this pagan Philistine too, for he has defied the armies of the living God! The Lord who rescued me from the claws of the lion and the bear will rescue me from this Philistine!' Saul finally consented. 'All right, go ahead,' he said. 'And may the Lord be with you!'"* [9]

David was secure in his ability to fight the giant. David was probably around 5'6" tall. The Philistine giant, Goliath, was somewhere between 6'6" and 9'9" tall.[10] Either way, we can assume that he was at the very least a foot taller than David. Goliath was also a seasoned warrior and very confident in his capabilities.

As I studied David and Goliath, I looked at the meaning of their names and realized their names alone tell part of their story. Personally, I never understood the power that resides within an individual's name because it was not part of my cultural experience. However, in the Jewish culture, names are very important. David means "Beloved"[11] and Goliath means "Exile: the exile; soothsayer, taken captive, stripped (as a captive)."[12] Let me put it this way, the beloved of God was looking at the one who was to be stripped of his perceived authority and taken captive.

Even with David's confidence in the Lord and in himself, his identity was still to be challenged.

> *"Then Saul gave David his own armor—a bronze helmet and a coat of mail, David put it on, strapped the sword over it, and took a step or two to see what it was like, for he had never worn such things before. 'I can't go in these,' he protested to Saul. 'I'm not used to them.' So David took them off again."* [13]

David tried to wear armor that wasn't made to fit him. This concept is vital. Whenever we put on a mask or pretend to be someone we are not, we veer from God's intended course. My identity was created uniquely for me, and your identity was created uniquely for you. They are not interchangeable.

When we enter a season of upgrade and transition, we are often tempted to put on another's armor. The key is what we do in that moment. David realized that he was putting on an identity that was not his (Saul's armor) and quickly took it off.

To walk into our own destiny, we must find our unique identity. As we discover our God-given identity, we will also find our individual strength.

UNLOCKING GREATNESS

It had been a difficult season, and it wasn't over. I decided to turn on the television and allow myself to be distracted for a bit. As I walked through the living room to pick up the TV remote, the Holy Spirit instructed me to look up Proverbs 3:5-6.

"Trust in and rely confidently on the Lord with all your heart and do not rely on your own insight or understanding. In all your ways know and acknowledge and recognize Him, And He will make your paths straight and smooth [removing obstacles that block your way]." [14]

Little did I know those words would quickly become a life verse for me. It would be something that I would hang onto for dear life as I moved through transition after transition, trial after trial, step after step trusting that God was positioning me for more. The challenge was, and still is, that I must do it His way, in His timing, and by His power not mine.

As David took off Saul's armor, he chose God's ammunition. David could only slay the giant with the tools and gifts that God had given him. In the natural, five smooth stones and a sling are not enough to defeat any giant. However, one shepherd boy, with radical faith in the Almighty God, proved it was more than enough.

"He picked up five smooth stones from a stream and put them into his shepherd's bag. Then, armed only with his shepherd's staff and sling, he started across the valley to fight the Philistine." [15]

With that one action David, the beloved, walked in his identity and did what no one else could do. He slew the giant, took back the ground that the enemy had stolen from Israel, and walked in victory. However, he had to do it without masking himself in Saul's identity (Saul's armor), amid disbelief and mockery (from his brothers), and in the order and timing that God orchestrated. David's strength was in the Lord which also implies that his identity was in the Lord.

One radically obedient individual following the one true God, always holds more than enough strength to conquer whatever is in front of them—even if it is a giant.

NECESSARY ENDINGS = GREAT BEGINNINGS

I mentioned earlier in this chapter that I had a severe speech impediment as a young child. When I was six years old, we moved from New York State to Michigan. To this day, I remember crying as we left the only town that I had ever known. I was as devastated as a six year old could be, and I do not doubt that I put my parents through all kinds of drama that went with that. What I didn't understand was that this move would have a powerful and strategic impact on my life.

At our little country school In Michigan, a speech therapist held the key to unlocking my speech patterns. I am sure that I learned numerous exercises to correct my speech; however, the only one that I remember is speaking into a cassette recorder and having to listen to myself talk, over and over and over. It is not easy to listen to a recording of yourself. However, if you want to improve, it is a necessary step. As I think about it, even that exercise was preparing me for what I am doing today but I didn't understand that at the tender age of six.

Throughout my life, God has brought about many necessary endings that also ultimately dealt with identity issues. Although necessary endings are not always easy, we can be assured that God will walk us through, mature us, and position us to go further than we ever imagined. And, as we make that journey, we can also rest assured that He is realigning our identity. The more we learn to see what He sees, the more we become like Him, and that includes how we see ourselves.

Another example of an identity challenge came from my senior pastor. I had just joined the pastoral staff at our church. Somehow,

I had to make a major transition from laity to pastoral staff. To say I was a bit uncomfortable and intimidated is an understatement. Like David, I had to learn to minister from who God made me to be, not wearing the mask of any other position or identity.

We were at a staff retreat when the senior pastor pulled me aside and said, "For us to see *you* as a pastor, you have to first see yourself as a pastor." God had called me into a season where part of my identity was to *be* a pastor. To walk into that role, I had to see myself through a different set of lenses and take on a distinct identity. Not to mention the fact that I had to deal with my own insecurities, masks, and false identities. I could not continue to wear a mask or walk in a false identity if I was to be a pastor to God's precious people. Oh, and did I mention that part of my job was to train and equip people to minister emotional healing to others? Talk about an eye-opening and challenging moment.

My identity was further challenged when, after years of walking in the calling of local pastoral ministry, God asked me to step down from that position. I was to pursue the call He had placed on my life and focus fulltime on His vision for Ruth Hendrickson Ministries. As I stepped into this transition, I distinctly heard the Lord saying to me that it was vital that I see myself in this new season as He sees me. It was essential that I allowed myself to dream with Him about what He was calling me into. I had to first take the ground in the spiritual realm, and see myself there, before I could walk it out in the physical. Another shift in my identity faced me. I had to learn to see myself and IDENTIFY myself as God did in every area of my life. I also had to understand that as I was growing in Him, my identity would also be expanding. Therefore, there would be identity shifts and increases that would come as I moved through various seasons of life.

As David tended sheep, was anointed by Samuel, tended more sheep, slayed Goliath and moved through all that stood in front of him, he was being prepared. God was positioning David to see himself as king. When David stood in front of Samuel to be anointed as king, he was not ready to take on that identity. Instead, God challenged him to take another step toward his intended future.

I am sure that David had doubts and fears like the rest of us do. Remember, he was human. David knew that in the good times and in the bad, he needed to grab hold of God. All that time hanging out in the fields with the sheep, he may have been forgotten by his family, but David had not been forgotten by God. In fact, David and God were developing a mighty relationship, which eventually led to David's journey along the road to the throne. He was not to become just another king but the greatest king that Israel had ever known.

"But now your (Saul) kingdom must end, for the Lord has sought out a man after his own heart. The Lord has already appointed him to be the leader of his people..." [16]

As we press through with God, He will do a major overhaul within us. And, I think we all understand by now that one of those areas that requires a major overhaul will be our identity. We are sons and daughters of the living God! We are heirs to the very Kingdom of Heaven. We are seated in heavenly places with Jesus, and so much more!

The invitation is open, ready and waiting. Your mission, should you choose to accept it, is to allow God to shift your identity to align with your position in Him and His plans and purposes for your life. Are you willing to walk into your destiny?

SPIRITUAL MUSCLE BUILDING

QUESTIONS

1. What is the mask(s) that you are wearing? Why have you felt it necessary to wear the mask?

2. What fears and insecurities do you have about taking the mask off? Be honest with the Lord and with yourself.

3. What can you do to embrace the necessary endings to make room for new beginnings? (Spend a few minutes with the Lord asking Him about this. You may be surprised what He shows you!)

ACTION STEPS

1. Research your name. What does it mean?

2. Give God permission to remove any masks and to begin to release your true identity.

3. Ask the Lord to share with you how He identifies you. Take time to listen and record what you hear.

4. Take time to worship and thank the Lord for what He is doing. Sing some Scripture such as Psalm 34:1-10.

PRAYER AND DECLARATION

Heavenly Father, I confess that portions of my true God-given identity have been lost. I also confess that there are times that I have put on a mask, therefore hiding the person You truly created me to be. I ask for Your forgiveness. Heavenly Father, I give You permission to help me remove the mask and to cleanse any area where I have held onto an identity that is incorrect or not mine to have.

Heavenly Father, I acknowledge that necessary endings can be challenging and difficult. I also acknowledge that at times I try to bring the past into my future. I release the past to You. I thank You for the many things that I have learned and the way that You will use those lessons as I walk into my future. I choose to align my focus with Your vision for my life and I will walk into the new season with joyous expectation.

It is my desire to walk in the fullness of who You created me to be. I declare that You know everything about me. I declare that I am created in Your image and that I carry Your DNA in the very core of my being. It is my desire to step into the fullness of that vision at Your perfect time. I declare that You have plans and purposes for me. I declare that as I trust in You and look to You that You will reveal the next step for me to take.

SCRIPTURAL BASIS:

Genesis 1:27, Psalm 139, Proverbs 3:5-6, 2 Corinthians 6:18

CHAPTER THREE

THE MAKING OF A WARDROBE

"I no longer merely confess that I am the righteousness of Christ. I realize that with His DNA in me through His blood, I could be nothing else. I realize the attributes of His DNA reside in me—whether dormant or active."[1]

CHE AHN

LA'BEL, *noun* A narrow slip of silk, paper or parchment, containing a name or title, and affixed to anything, denoting its contents. Such are the labels affixed to the vessels of an apothecary. Labels also are affixed to deeds or writings to hold the appended seal.[2]

Ruth's Version: I like the above definition because Webster uses the analogy of labels affixed to a prescription bottle. That is something we can all relate to. The label describes what is inside the bottle. As we navigate through this section I would encourage you to be asking Holy Spirit to reveal:

1. What labels are affixed to me?

2. Are the labels that are affixed to me healthy/godly or unhealthy/ungodly?

STICKY MOMENTS

If I were to say that I detest math, it would not be a strong enough statement. Math, in and of itself, cannot make me like or dislike it. However, my personal experiences with math were extremely negative and, unfortunately, left a lasting negative impact.

When I was in elementary school, a chart was hung on the wall to teach the students multiplication. The teacher didn't realize that I became so adept at reading the chart, that I didn't learn how to do the math. Therefore, when they took down the chart that I had so wonderfully mastered, I was in serious trouble. In hindsight, that should have been a warning for my parents of what was to come.

Before I share my next experience, let me set the stage. I have only one sibling, and she is four years older than I am and is a math whiz. We grew up in a little town in Michigan where our school system was extremely small. Therefore, we had only one math teacher in the entire high school. The area was a vast farming community, and I don't think they gave much thought to college-bound students. The school only offered basic algebra and geometry courses. However, my sister, the math whiz, convinced the teacher to allow her to self-study and take calculus, at which she naturally excelled and easily understood.

When I entered high school, I, too, had to take the required math courses. What I didn't realize was that the years of math would be the least of my issues. I would come face-to-face with a teacher who had cast me as another math whiz, and who would consistently demean me and refuse to help me when I didn't live up to her expectation. The ridicule from this teacher further solidified the labeling that had begun in elementary school—that I could not do the math, that I wasn't as smart as my sister, that I was stupid. To top it off, she gave me two deficiency reports during those four years, which added to my shame.

As we walk through life, we pick up labels that try to define us. It's not uncommon to feel these labels are glued on with epoxy. An epoxy is a two-part high-performance bonding system that was created for use in extreme environments. Part one of the epoxy is that we receive the label. The label may be a positive (Godly), life-giving label, or it may be negative (ungodly) label that holds us back due to pain, fear, etc. Part two of the epoxy is the reinforcement of that label. Each time a label is reinforced, the bond becomes stronger, eventually becoming an identity.

Reinforced negative labels often go underground, their high sticky value subtly becoming a hindrance to our walking in the full confidence that God intends for us. Whereas, positive labels have the potential to propel us forward. The sticky value for the negative label applied by my math teacher increased over time as I believed the lie that I couldn't understand math, that I was stupid, etc. As I mentioned previously, the glue for labels is like a two-part epoxy. The first part of the glue was applied in elementary school without my realizing it. But the elementary school labels provided the perfect reinforcement for the second part of the process. As I hit high school, the second part of the process found its base and became an effective adhesion that would impact me for years to come.

There is a little term that I have coined called *sticky value*. Think of trying to remove a price tag. Sometimes they come off very easily leaving no residue. This morning, however, I picked up a hand mirror that I had recently purchased, and after attempting to take off the price tag, I found that it could not be removed easily. I scraped and scraped but the residue remained. And to make matters worse, there were two other labels on the mirror that simply would not rub off either. Some labels have a low sticky value while others have a very high sticky value.

In the same way, we all wear unhealthy-ungodly labels that have a low sticky value and can come off easily. And then there are other labels that leave a residue that seems impossible to remove. We need the Holy Spirit to gently remove that residue and set us free. On the other end of the spectrum, we each have godly labels in our lives that seem to blow away as if they didn't have enough adhesive to make them stick in the first place. Those labels need increased sticky value. Fortunately, we also have godly labels with a strong adhesive, areas where we can rejoice in what God has done in our lives.

There is always an ongoing battle for control of our minds. Even when dealing with labels, God is still asking the same question. *Do you see what I see?* Just as that negative label was being applied to me, there were also very positive labels reinforced through the same school system. Although I struggled with math, I excelled at many other things. I did well with other subjects; I was social and outgoing; I was an athletic trainer, served on student council, and became president of the National Honor Society, eventually graduating with honors.

My parents never figured out, nor did I, how I could receive two deficiency reports, pass math by the skin of my teeth, and yet be president of the National Honor Society and graduate with honors.

God indeed works in mysterious ways. And fortunately for me, He sometimes does math the same way I do.

THE GOD FACTOR

In the 1980's, there was a song that frequently played on the radio. I don't remember the title nor the group that performed it. However, there is one line of that song that has stayed with me over the years: *"When He looks at me, He sees not what I used to be, but He sees Jesus."*[3]

I have many favorite stories in the Bible. However, Gideon, as he partners with God to solve math and warfare issues together, is undoubtedly at the top of the list. I am sure you have figured out by now that identity, belief systems, and labels are intertwined and work in partnership with each other. Gideon struggled with all of these and yet had a powerful experience as he trusted God for each step he took.

We meet Gideon in Judges 6. At this point in Israel's history, they were being oppressed by the Midianites. *"The Midianites were so cruel that the Israelites made hiding places for themselves in the mountains, caves, and strongholds."*[4] In the midst of this cruelty, the Israelites needed to find creative ways to provide for themselves. Gideon had a winepress and hid there to thrash his wheat. Many a sermon has condemned Gideon for his actions as they focus on the word *hiding*; however, I would suggest that it was quite possibly a wonderful God-given idea. Sometimes we miss the very thing that God puts in front of us that will move us to the next level of our journey.

Furthermore, *"the angel of the Lord came and sat."*[5] This tells me that God can and will find us even when we hide. The Psalmist reminds us, *"I can never escape from your Spirit! I can never get away from your presence."* [6] We need to understand that this is true physically and spiritually. And, God is always willing to deal with our negative and unhealthy labels. With that said, let me remind you that He is also working to reinforce our good, godly labels.

I wonder if Gideon wore the label of *victim*. Remember, his people were subject to the Midianites and experienced extreme cruelty. When the angel greeted Gideon, two very specific things are stated. First, Gideon was greeted as a *mighty hero.*[7] The angel was speaking prophetically into Gideon's intended future. In other words, through God's eyes, Gideon was on the winning side.

Secondly, the angel gave Gideon a reminder that the Lord was with him.[8] Gideon's response was a prime example of the godly labels being unable to adhere immediately because the sticky value of the unhealthy labels is so strong. Gideon questioned the Lord's presence and the lack of miracles. God will go to great lengths to redefine us. I love how Scripture reads:

> *"Then the Lord turned to him and said, 'Go with the strength you have and rescue Israel from the Midianites. I am sending you!'"* [9]

God wasn't concerned about Gideon's questions or his labels. God was looking at the abilities that He had placed within Gideon. God had every intention of sending the full power and backing of the Kingdom of Heaven with Gideon. However, just as it often happens with us, Gideon hadn't caught on yet.

For whatever reason, Gideon also believed he was from the weakest clan and was the least in his entire family.[10] Within many families, there are both spoken and unspoken expectations and comparisons of children. The result of this is that many of us have compared ourselves to others, and judged ourselves to be less than. If I feel inadequate, I tend to get quiet, while others may get loud and demand attention.

Gideon carried on a conversation with the Lord. This is key because that conversation led to a change in his labeling system. The conversation between Gideon and the Lord opened the doors for Gideon to explore his relationship with God. From destroying his father's idols[11] to the famous story of the fleeces,[12] God patiently showed Gideon that both the idols (anything that stood between God and His children) and the labels were being removed. One patient step at a time, God asked Gideon, "Do you see what I see?"

God consistently called Gideon a "mighty warrior" and provided Gideon opportunities to walk in that identity. That choice didn't always come easily. Gideon asked God to confirm what He was saying not only once but twice. With each new opportunity, God took Gideon a giant step further in the development of his identity. If Gideon only saw himself hiding in a winepress with no power or authority, he would never see himself as a mighty warrior. God never changed how *He* saw Gideon, but Gideon's focus had to change to align with God's.

As we began talking about Gideon, I mentioned math. The other thing that God was going to teach Gideon was that man's mathematics and methods of warfare do not always align with God's math and methods.

Gideon was redefined to the extent that he was ready to go to war. As a good leader, he sounded the alarm and the army gathered. As they began to march, God suddenly declared a need to downsize. According to God's instructions, Gideon told the people, "'*Whoever is timid or afraid may leave this mountain and go home.' So 22,000 of them went home, leaving only 10,000 who were willing to fight."*[13] God further sent home another 9,700 leaving 300 to battle against an army of 135,000 Midianites.

Just to clarify, that is a difference of 134,700 warriors. In other words, the Israelites were outnumbered 450 to 1. From a strategic perspective, the Midianites would be victorious; however, with God in the equation, everything would change.

We all like to think that we are brave and willing to step out. God had to remind Gideon over and over that He was there to help. Friends have conversations and Gideon had not been abandoned by God. God continued His conversation with Gideon as the army's size was reduced. God continued to remove Gideon's old labels and adhere his new labels with glue straight from the Kingdom of Heaven. God basically sent Gideon into the enemy camp to hear about a dream and its interpretation, which made no sense in the natural, yet made perfect sense in God's way of thinking.

> *"That night the Lord said, 'Get up! Go down into the Midianite camp, for I have given you victory over them! But if you are afraid to attack, go down to the camp with your servant Purah. Listen to what the Midianites are saying, and you will be greatly encouraged. Then you will be eager to attack.' So Gideon took Purah and went down to the edge of the enemy camp. The armies of Midian, Amalek, and the people of the east had settled in the valley like a swarm of locusts. Their camels were like grains of sand on the seashore — too many to count!*

> *"Gideon crept up just as a man was telling his companion about a dream. The man said, 'I had this dream, and in my dream*

a loaf of barley bread came tumbling down in the Midianite camp. It hit a tent, turned it over, and knocked it flat!' His companion answered, 'Your dream can mean only one thing — God has given Gideon son of Joash, the Israelite, victory over Midian and all its allies!'" [14]

In summary, God chose a man who was hiding in a winepress who believed he was the least. God called him into his destiny. However, to get there, Gideon had to release his old belief patterns, identity, and labels, and allow God to redefine him. Gideon also had to see himself through God's eyes, take a risk, and do the impossible. The result was freedom for him and for his people.

It can be easy to read a good story and not put yourself in the middle of it. I'm pretty sure I would have been terrified as I compared my small group of men to the vast Midianite army. Fear would have been banging on my door. I am also sure that I would have questioned if I had even heard God in the first place. However, God will always take us further than we believe we can go and give us a more significant impact than we believe we can have.

Do I recognize God's voice when He speaks to me?

Have I learned to have conversations with God about my identity and my destiny?

Even as you ask questions, understand that you are always in a learning process. If you don't feel like you have learned to converse with God, don't worry! Give yourself lots of grace in the process. It takes time but don't wait. In fact, today is a great time to start. Just ask the Holy Spirit to show you some of the ways God has spoken to you in the past. You'll be amazed at how active God has been in your life. Never discount Scriptures that He brings to mind. Remember that the Word of God is alive and active, and His Scripture is just one of the ways that God speaks to you.

Now, take a few minutes, sit back and have a conversation with Him. Talk for a bit and listen for a bit. He really is a great conversationalist.

FOOT IN MOUTH SYNDROME

Peter is another one of my favorite people in Scripture. Why? Probably because Peter is adept at sticking his foot in his mouth. In other words, he tends to speak before he fully thinks things through. If you cannot relate to the foot in mouth syndrome, I am sure you can think of someone who fits the description.

In Matthew 16, Jesus asks the disciples who people think He is. From that point, Jesus narrowed it down even further and asked the disciples directly who they thought He was. Don't be fooled; Jesus already knew all their answers. I believe He was challenging the disciples' hearts by providing them with an invitation to look deeply into their core belief system. As I read the account, I thought back to various meetings I have been in where a question is asked, and an awkward silence fills the room. I am guessing that there was a moment of silence until Peter blurted out, *"... 'You are the Christ (the Messiah, the Anointed), the Son of the living God.'"*[15]

It is at this very juncture where Jesus puts a powerful new label on Peter.

> *"Then Jesus answered him, 'Blessed [happy, spiritually secure, favored by God] are you, Simon son of Jonah, because flesh and blood (mortal man) did not reveal this to you, but My Father who is in heaven. And I say to you that you are Peter, and on this rock I will build My church; and the gates of Hades (death) will*

THE MAKING OF A WARDROBE

*not overpower it [by preventing the resurrection of the Christ].
I will give you the keys (authority) of the kingdom of heaven;
and whatever you bind [forbid, declare to be improper and
unlawful] on earth will have [already] been bound in heaven,
and whatever you loose [permit, declare lawful] on earth will
have [already] been loosed in heaven.'"* [16]

Put yourself in Peter's shoes. I am sure he was bursting with joy.
And probably yelling, "UPGRADE!" Jesus had just given him a
promotion to church builder.

Think back over your life. How many times have you experienced a
spiritual mountaintop just to find yourself cast down into the valley?

Growing up in Michigan, we had iced toboggan runs (think bobsled
run). You climb up to the top, dressed in a heavy snowmobile suit,
boots, gloves, and hat. You get seated on the toboggan and with a
push, you are off. The wind whips your face; tears form from the
cold; you shift and lean trying to go as fast as you can, all the while
giving a whoop and a holler. Before you know it, you are tumbling off
the toboggan, realizing that your pants got singed from the friction
on the way down. Oh well, the ride was worth it!

Peter has this amazing mountaintop exchange with Jesus, yells
UPGRADE. Almost immediately, he plunges into the valley with
burn marks on his britches.

Jesus talked with His disciples about His death. He did not want them
to be caught off-guard, nor did He want them to fall. When we listen
to Him, He is still guiding our steps, filling in the blanks, helping us
to understand, and desiring that we, too, won't fall. However, like
Peter, there are times when we just don't get it. I have to wonder if
the human side of Jesus wasn't processing with His disciples as He

shared with them what was about to happen, that He would be taken to Jerusalem, suffer, be crucified, and then raised from the dead.

> *"Peter took Him aside [to speak to Him privately] and began to reprimand Him, saying, 'May God forbid it! This will never happen to You.' But Jesus turned and said to Peter, 'Get behind Me, Satan! You are a stumbling block to Me; for you are not setting your mind on things of God, but on things of man.'"* [17]

Peter, full of faith and bursting at the seams from his previous conversation, speaks out with confidence and boldness, only to have Jesus rebuke him. Ouch! At this point, Peter could have taken on a very negative label. I cannot imagine having Jesus look at me and say, "Get away from me" let alone call me "Satan". If we do not hold those statements within the whole counsel of Scripture, the concept will mess with our theology.

When we are dropping from the mountain top to the valley, we have a decision to make. We need to understand that we determine if we get burned, battered and broken in the descent or if we stand victorious.

> Properly handled, a trek to the valley becomes
> a stepping stone to our next mountaintop.

I would suggest that Peter's sticky value was coated with the very essence of God's love. He received assurance and confidence as Jesus declared his future as the foundation on which the church would be built. Peter's faith soared as he realized that anything the demonic would throw at the church would not have the power to overthrow His kingdom.

"'For I know the plans I have for you,' says the Lord. 'They are plans for good and not for disaster, to give you a future and a hope.'" [18]

Remember that two-part epoxy? Peter's declaration of Jesus' identity, *"You are the Messiah, the Son of the living God."* [19] was the first part of the epoxy. As Jesus not only confirmed the declaration but prophesied Peter's future, the second part of the epoxy was activated, and the bond strengthened. With that assurance of faith and trust in his Savior, the rebuke from Jesus could not become anything other than an invitation to grow and journey with Him. If you know the continuing saga of Peter's life, you understand that the journey was full of ups and downs. However, in the end, the labels Peter wore were all superglued with epoxy straight from the throne room of heaven.

Have we believed the epoxy and labels for our lives from our perceived failures, words and demonic interference—or—are we using epoxy and heavenly labels that have been purchased by Jesus Christ at an exceedingly great price?

GOD'S LABEL MAKER

Years ago, as a shift was coming in my life, I sat with one of my mentors who asked a question that would adhere to my very soul and become a part of my plumb-line with God. The question was, "What makes your heart sing?" I remember reading somewhere that if you have a dream that you can accomplish on your own, it is probably not a God dream.

Along with the impossible dreams that we dream with God, I would also suggest that there is a song that rises in our hearts as we walk with God. When we nurture the song and allow it to grow in the recesses of our heart, it also becomes a solvent that challenges and dissolves the negative labels that have adhered to our very beings. As the ungodly labels dissolve, our God-given dreams, focus, and destiny rise to the surface unhindered as His song blesses that which God has placed within us.

> I love seeing the light go on in people's lives…that precious moment when they see and understand that they can do what God is calling them to do. It's so amazing and makes my heart sing.

Just like God spoke to Gideon and restored Peter, He will confirm the identity that He has placed within you. For me, He did it through numerous prophetic words. Occasionally, God brought a prophet around who would speak directly to me. It was like pouring God's living water on the dream that marinated within the very core of my being for years. The best way to describe it is to take a perfectly cut steak and letting it marinate in the savoriest of seasonings. After it sits for a while, you cook it while enjoying the wonderful aroma and look forward to the delicious morsels to come. (Sorry, all you nonmeat-eaters. I give you full license to switch the wording to something involving veggies that will work for you!)

That is what happens when you are carefully tending a "God dream". We do have permission to daydream with God. I would sit and wonder what it would be like to walk into my God-given purpose and destiny. As I dreamed with God, I asked Him to prepare me. I spent several years marinating before God released me to walk into my destiny.

However, during those years He was doing a major overhaul on the labels that I had worn. For years, I was told that I was not enough. It wasn't always spoken in those terms, but it is what I heard through the lenses that I had developed. I had to choose to see myself as the person God was calling me to be. I had to believe that He was willing and able to position me to walk into my divine destiny. I had to be able to answer the "Do you see what I see?" question with a resounding YES. But that journey took time.

When God redefines you, the sticky value of His labels is massive. It will make the most steadfast adhesive on those pesky, unhealthy and ungodly labels look weak.

We have talked about Gideon and Peter. However, before we conclude this chapter, I would be remiss if I didn't bring Jabez into the story. In many ways, he was an amazing example of dealing with the sticky value of labels.

Scripture frequently reminds us that the meaning of a person's name has been important throughout the centuries. For a moment, put yourself in the shoes of Jabez. This poor fellow's name means, "*He will cause pain; whiteness swept away; mire swept away; shovel of mire.*"[20] We all know what pain is, but these parents branded their child with being the cause of pain. Let's go a step deeper with the definition. What about the word *mire*? One definition for mire, according to Merriam-Webster is, "*a troublesome or intractable situation.*"[21] Not only was Jabez named as one who would cause pain, but he was also labeled a troublesome situation.

I have given birth to five children. As much as people claim you will forget the pain of childbirth, you don't. Giving birth is painful. However, it would have never dawned on me to give any of my kids a name that reflected the pain of childbirth. All I can say is that Jabez must have had a unique mother, for at the moment of his birth, she gave him a name meaning pain! But it is vital to note that Jabez didn't allow that label to adhere and become his identity.

> *"Now Jabez was more honorable than his brothers, and his mother called his name Jabez, saying, 'Because I bore him in pain.' And Jabez called on the God of Israel saying, 'Oh, that You would bless me indeed, and enlarge my territory, that Your hand would be with me, and that You would keep me from evil, that I may not cause pain!' So God granted him what he requested."* [22]

The very first thing I notice is that Jabez grew up to be an honorable man. Not only an honorable man, but more honorable than his brothers. Scripture doesn't go into detail with this, but I wonder what the backstory was. There had to be a significant difference between Jabez and his brothers to be stated explicitly in Scripture. I would suggest that, at the very least, honor became a healthy label that adhered to his identity. I believe this because, of everything that Scripture could have pointed out about Jabez, God chose to highlight that he was honorable. It is clear that Jabez realized what he was and what he was not. He was a man who desired to have impact. This is shown in the prayer for his territory to be enlarged. However, he also desired to be kept from evil and not cause pain to anyone else. That is honor.

The other thing I noticed is that Jabez took the label of *pain* and turned it around. Rev. Charles Cooper states that the name Jabez was actually *nonsense* in Hebrew, that his mother used a pun to make up his name.[2] In Hebrew, Jabez (*yabez*) and the term for pain (*ozeb*) have the last three letters switched. This pun on pain is used as a tool to explain the circumstances of the child's birth.

Pun or not, if he were born today, I can hear the kids on the playground taunting him, teasing him about his name and reminding him daily how much pain he caused. One of the few memories I have of kindergarten is being teased because I couldn't speak correctly. At that time, I was too young to know how to process this, or to even know that I needed to take it to God. It was an area where I needed His healing and allow Him to redefine me. As adults, we can still experience various forms of taunting and teasing. The challenge is to cry out to God in the midst of those moments, and allow Him to define us.

As I write this, we live on the other side of the Cross from where Jabez lived. We have the fullness of Scripture that Jabez didn't have. As Jesus was nailed to the Cross, He carried every curse that had come upon humanity. Scripture tells us that Jesus rescued us from the curse when he hung on the Cross.[24] In other words, every wound, every negative label, every curse is not ours to carry. The taunting words from my younger years were not meant to define my life, neither are the negative words spoken over you or your negative experiences intended to define yours. The question is who/what are you allowing to label you?

We don't know how old Jabez was when he prayed his now famous prayer. However, we do know that it echoed through the very halls of heaven and the mandate was given to record it in the Bible as a lesson for generations to come.

Jabez prayed for more! Scripture is very clear that his request was directed solely to the God of Israel. In the midst of the stories, teasing, and taunting that probably happened, Jabez made a significant decision. He prayed! He prayed that the circumstances that had surrounded his birth and his name would not characterize his life or be a prophetic indicator of his future.

Each of us has a choice.
Do we live *to* the labels or *beyond* the labels?
Do we live *to* our name or *beyond* our name?

Some labels are easy to throw off while others are difficult. Some are so deeply ingrained that they first need the healing touch of Jesus. We need Him to remove the negative label and allow Him to rebrand us with His label from the very throne room of heaven. And then, we must learn to walk in that new identity. Walking in that new identity means that we take on that new identity in thought, word, and action.

In summary, as God transforms our life, unhealthy and ungodly labels need to be removed, and healing brought forth. Sometimes behavior patterns that have been driven by a label need to change as we walk in our healing. In the natural, if we take a blow dryer and blow heat on the label, it will eventually loosen and come off. When we allow God to blow His refining fire on our unhealthy and ungodly labels, we can rest assured that all traces of those labels will be removed and disappear. God will brand us with His label, our true identity, making it possible for us to be strategically positioned to move into the fullness of all He has for us.

Gideon, Peter, and Jabez all were confronted in different ways concerning their identity. Each one chose to walk with the Lord.

SPIRITUAL MUSCLE BUILDING

QUESTIONS

1. What is my sticky value?

2. What unhealthy or ungodly labels have I picked up over the years that are stuck to me?

3. What are the corresponding behavior patterns that need to change?

4. What are the good and godly labels that have attached to me?

ACTION STEPS

1. Find a quiet place and spend time with the Lord. Ask His forgiveness for picking up the unhealthy or ungodly labels and corresponding behavioral patterns.

2. As you are sitting with the Lord, ask Him how He sees you. If you feel like you don't hear anything, no worries. Go to Action Step 3 and declare that Scripture over your life.

3. Read Psalm 139:1-18.

4. Take time to worship. If you desire, you can take Psalm 139:1-18 and re-write it in your own words as a song of thanksgiving.

PRAYER AND DECLARATION

Heavenly Father, You have created me to be loved, valued and priceless. You have created me in Your image. I ask Your forgiveness for the times that I have knowingly or unknowingly accumulated labels that do not align with Your view of me. Not only do they not align, but they also cover up who You created me to be. I give You permission to remove the ungodly labels and to restore the identity that You have created for me.

I declare that You have placed Your DNA within me. I declare that I reflect the glory of my heavenly Father. I declare that what will stick to me is the identity that You have created me to be clothed in. I declare that I no longer wear the garments of a slave, but I wear the garments of an heir to the Kingdom of Heaven. I declare that I am a dearly loved child of the Living God.

I declare that the labels that I will wear are straight from You. Heavenly Father, I ask that You pour Your oil over me so that nothing can adhere that is not from You.

SCRIPTURAL BASIS:

Genesis 1:27, Romans 8:17, Galatians 3:29, Galatians 4:7

CHAPTER FOUR
DANGEROUS CAVERNS

"Give me one hundred preachers who fear nothing but sin and desire nothing but God, and I care not whether they be clergymen or laymen, they alone will shake the gates of Hell and set up the Kingdom of Heaven upon Earth."[1]
JOHN WESLEY

FEAR, *noun.* A painful emotion or passion excited by an expectation of evil, or the apprehension of impending danger. *Fear* expresses less apprehension than dread, and dread less than terror and fright.[2]

INSECU'RITY, *noun* [in and security.] Want of safety or want of confidence in safety. Seamen in a tempest must be conscious of their *insecurity.*

Uncertainty. With what *insecurity* of truth we ascribe effects or unseen causes.[3]

Ruth's Short Version: When I think of fear and insecurity I think of "kissing cousins." Taken down to the bare bones, the term kissing cousins means one that is closely related in kind to something else.[4] Fear and insecurity usually travel together and if left to their own devices will eventually create a cavern that is deep, dark and ugly.

As we journey through this chapter, remember that we were not created to live in fear and insecurity. As the prophet Isaiah so aptly reminds us,

> "But those who wait for the Lord [who expect, look for, and hope in Him] Will gain new strength and renew their power; They will lift up their wings [and rise up close to God] like eagles [rising toward the sun]; They will run and not become weary; They will walk and not grow tired."[5]

NAY-SAYERS, WHAT-IF, AND IF ONLY

While sinkholes are common in many regions, they are not that common in New Jersey where we live. However, some time ago my husband's excavation company was contracted to remedy a sinkhole. The sinkhole had already compromised a swimming pool and was working its way toward the house.

The type of sinkhole that typically makes newspaper headlines is referred to as a cover-collapse sinkhole. Simply put, there are small cracks and voids beneath the earth's surface that become hollowed out by water erosion. Over time, the cover (the earth's surface) remains intact, with no visible evidence of what is occurring underground. However, as the hole becomes larger, the ground cover cannot support its own weight, so it collapses forming a sinkhole. As it collapses, whatever was sitting on, or was built upon the surface drops into the hole.

How many of us can relate to walking along, life going amazingly well, when suddenly the proverbial rug is pulled out from under us? Suddenly, we find ourselves falling into a sinkhole that we never realized was there, tumbling downward, wondering where the bottom is and if we will survive the fall. Fear and insecurity can become the cinder blocks wrapped around us, dragging us deeper than we ever imagined we could go.

The prophet Elijah seemed to have a track record of living with an emotional roller-coaster that periodically stopped and invited fear and insecurity along for the ride.

In 1 Kings 18, Elijah is embroiled in the famous battle with the prophets of Baal. In short, Ahab is king, and there is a severe famine in the land. After a few years, God sends Elijah to deliver a message to Ahab that rain is coming. Ahab's greeting reminds us that Ahab and Elijah were not on good terms. *"So, is it really you, you troublemaker of Israel?"*[6] Of course, Elijah responds that the king and his family have caused the trouble for Israel. I find it interesting that God sends Elijah to deliver a message concerning rain. However, before the rain can begin, there first had to be an epic battle of the gods.

The people are called together and the prophets of Baal summoned. The altars are built, and the sacrificial bulls are slaughtered. The catch—which god will set the wood on fire? The prophets of Baal shout, cut themselves, and rave with no response from Baal. Elijah tells the people to pour water over his offering a number of times, so everything is well saturated. He then prayed.

"Immediately, the fire of the Lord flashed down from heaven and burned up the young bull, the wood, the stones, and the dust. It even licked up all the water in the trench! And when all the

*people saw it, they fell face down on the ground and cried out,
'the Lord – He is God! Yes, the Lord is God!'"* [7]

A winner is declared and the epic battle is over. However, was the
battle really over for Elijah? Remember why God sent him? He
brought a message that rain was coming. Elijah turns back to the
task at hand and begins to pray for rain.

*"And soon the sky was black with clouds. A heavy wind brought
a terrific rainstorm, and Ahab left quickly for Jezreel."* [8]

Elijah was a prophet who knew God, heard His voice, and delivered
His messages. He saw signs, wonders, and miracles. He was not afraid
of the king, the people, or the four hundred prophets of Baal that he
challenged. He was confident in the power of God as he had water
dumped on the sacrifice and the wooden altar before asking God to
light it on fire. If you have ever tried to start a fire with damp or soggy
wood, you'll know that it doesn't work too well.

But Elijah was still human. For whatever reason, there was a dangerous
sinkhole or cavern in his life that he was about to fall into because
this mighty prophet was deathly afraid of a woman. She brought out
all his issues of fear and insecurity.

*"When Ahab got home, he told Jezebel everything Elijah had
done, including the way he had killed all the prophets of Baal.
So Jezebel sent this message to Elijah: 'May the gods strike me
and even kill me if by this time tomorrow I have not killed you
just as you killed them.' Elijah was afraid and fled for his life."* [9]

Elijah hits a proverbial low point. He immediately forgets about his
relationship with God, the torrential rainstorm that God had sent,
the victory over the prophets of Baal and seeing God set fire to the

altar. Instead, he takes himself into the wilderness, sits down and prays to die. The good thing is that God knows exactly where each of us are, even at the lowest of lows in the middle of a desert. The angel of the Lord provided food and sent Elijah to Mount Sinai. When he reached Mount Sinai, he went into a cave to spend the night.[10]

I remember taking my kids to see one of the caverns near our home. At one point, they turned out the lights so we could experience what it is like to have the total absence of light in the physical world. It was so dark that we could not see our hands in front of our faces, which also meant that I could not see my children, the tour guide, or the sides of the cavern. I quickly realized that if I moved, I could step off the ledge. Suddenly, I found myself feeling isolated and alone, with no sense of direction.

In the spiritual realm, we are on extremely dangerous ground when we enter those spiritual caves and caverns. They are places where we feel isolated with no sense of direction. The darkness is so dense that we cannot see or sense anything but impending doom. As J.I. Packer states, "Disregard the study of God, and you sentence yourself to stumble and blunder through life blindfolded, as it were, with no sense of direction and no understanding of what surrounds you."[11]

When we enter spiritual caves and caverns, we open the door for fear and insecurity to come raging into our lives. We run the risk of aborting our God-ordained future.

When we enter these pitch-black caverns, the lie has the potential to speak louder than the truth. God finds Elijah in the cave and calls him back to the mountain. It is on the mountain where God reminds Elijah whom he serves. God will always meet us in the caves and caverns of our lives and ask us why we are there.

As followers of Jesus, we were created to live in the light, not in the darkness. The truth is that when we are walking with God, there is no place where we can truly hide. He always knows where we are. He doesn't send out a search party. He comes into those places Himself. The lie tells us we are alone. However, the truth is that He will never leave us or forsake us.[12] Another way to put that is that no matter where we wander, He will never walk away and leave us. Even in the darkest moments, we are never alone. In those dark moments, don't trust your feelings; trust what God has promised. He will lead you out into His light.

> *"'Go out and stand before me on the mountain,' the Lord told him. And as Elijah stood there, the Lord passed by, and a mighty windstorm hit the mountain. It was such a terrible blast that the rocks were torn loose, but the Lord was not in the wind. After the wind there was an earthquake, but the Lord was not in the earthquake. And after the earthquake there was a fire, but the Lord was not in the fire. And after the fire there was the sound of a gentle whisper. When Elijah heard it, he wrapped his face in his cloak and went out and stood at the entrance of the cave. And a voice said, 'What are you doing here, Elijah?'"* [13]

As Elijah pours out his heart to God, I hear frustration and tiredness in Elijah's words. He is afraid, tired and believes that he is alone. In other words, he is battling feelings of hopelessness, depression and wanting to die. When we are afraid and insecure, our vision becomes skewed. As the conversation continues, God tells Elijah that he has seven-thousand others who have not worshipped Baal.[14]

At the end of the conversation, God gives Elijah a to-do list including the commissioning of his replacement. Some commentators believe that this was God's love being poured out on Elijah by giving him a companion. We see this modeled in the New Testament as Jesus sends out the disciples in groups of two, and spoken of in the Old Testament.

"Two people are better off than one, for they can help each other succeed. If one person falls, the other can reach out and help. But someone who falls alone is in real trouble." [15]

When we try to hide our fear and insecurities, eventually things reach a tipping point and the surface covering caves in just like a sinkhole. Suddenly, we find ourselves falling further and going deeper into the hole than we ever imagined. Elijah put his focus on the woman, Jezebel, rather than the Lord. He didn't need to run to the desert, and he didn't need to pray to die. He needed to ask God for strength and wisdom and trust the mighty God whom he served to spread protection over him.

"But let them all be glad, those who turn aside to hide themselves in You. May they keep shouting for joy forever! Overshadow them in Your presence as they sing and rejoice. Then every lover of Your name will burst forth with endless joy." [16]

Like Elijah, it is not uncommon for all of this to hit after a significant God victory. But remember, we were not created to live in isolation but in community. When we walk together, we can go further than we can go alone, and it is more difficult for fear and insecurity to take control.

BUILDING BLOCKS

I think almost every child has played with building blocks. According to an expert in child development, benefits of building blocks include: hand-eye coordination, early math and engineering skills, spatial awareness, fine motor skills and logical thinking. [17] As adults, we still play with building blocks, just in a more mature form, such as Jenga or other similar games.

Every time I walk into our basement, I am reminded of building blocks. My home has a basement with cinder block walls. When the house was built, a mason had to know how to properly set the cinder blocks to provide the structural strength needed to build the walls. If the blocks were not set correctly, they would not be able to support the weight of the structure that is built on top. If a load-bearing wall (such as your foundation wall) begins to bow, there must be additional support structures added.

Spiritually, fear and anxiety enter when our foundational building blocks are not correctly aligned. Quite often, we will try to fix the foundation with sub-standard materials. We must remember that we serve the Master Creator who can make all things new.[18]

Today, people in many countries are not familiar with walled cities. When we think of a wall, it is either cement blocks like I described above, the wall of a house, the Wailing Wall in Jerusalem, or maybe a decorative wall that defines a boundary line. However, there are times when a wall is much more than a foundation or boundary. There are times when a wall is the defensive "weapon" that wraps around a city. Such was the case in Nehemiah's day.

We need to recognize that God will often put us in positions that will call us to more. Nehemiah was a man who stepped into that call and didn't allow the dangerous cavern of fear and insecurity to get a foothold.

Nehemiah was an official in the court of King Artaxerxes. Since King Artaxerxes was a Persian king, we know that Nehemiah was not in his homeland but living in captivity. Scripture tells us that Nehemiah served as the king's cupbearer.[19] God strategically placed Nehemiah in a position that would radically impact His people. Like the chess master or tapestry weaver, God was making moves that would bring everything together.

As Nehemiah served the king, he usually served with joy. However, one day, he was sad. *"So the king asked me, 'Why are you looking so sad? You don't look sick to me. You must be deeply troubled.'"*[20] I love how Scripture is transparent and doesn't cover up. The New Living Translation states that Nehemiah was terrified.[21] However, what I notice with Nehemiah is that the terror didn't become a sinkhole; instead it became a bridge to wall building.

The bridge is the prayer that Nehemiah frantically sent up to the heavens as he addressed the king. *"The king asked, 'Well, how can I help you?' With a prayer to the God of heaven, I replied..."*[22] Nehemiah didn't allow his focus to be drawn away from the One who was ultimately in control. In fact, it's possible that the frantic prayer consisted of one word. "Help!"

It's important to note that Nehemiah had already spent time in mourning, fasting, and prayer concerning the situation in Judah.[23] He had already turned his heart to God, and he maintained that position before the king and with that, God gave him favor. Not only favor, but exceedingly abundant favor. Nehemiah's first request was just for time off to rebuild Judah. However, as he and the king conversed, Nehemiah walked into a season of favor with the king and was able to ask for letters that would ultimately give him the much-needed supplies for his assignment. And then the king went another step further and provided army officers and horsemen to protect him during his journey.[24]

With every word, directive, or action of God, there is also a time component. Stepping out of God's timing opens the door for fear and insecurity to slide in. The remnant of people who had remained in Jerusalem were living in such fear and insecurity. Because of this, they were unable to repair the wall or move forward with their lives. All they could see was the hopelessness and despair within their ruined city. Nehemiah kept himself separate as he inspected the wall and reached out for God's plans from the Throne Room of Heaven. He maintained his perspective, focus, and sensitivity to God's appropriate timing.

We are reminded to *"Be well balanced and always alert, because your enemy, the devil, roams around incessantly, like a roaring lion looking for its prey to devour."* [25] One of the keys to walking out of fear and insecurity is choosing whose voice you are going to listen to. The primary battle will happen in your mind. However, there are also times when those negative voices will manifest.

As Nehemiah began to unfold the plan and engage the city officials, there was considerable excitement. Nehemiah's focus never shifted; he knew it was time; he knew it was God's plan; and he knew that God would protect him. Therefore, fear and insecurity were locked out from Nehemiah's life.

> *"But when Sanballat, Tobiah, and Geshem the Arab heard of our plan, they scoffed contemptuously. 'What are you doing? Are you rebelling against the king?' they asked."* [26]

Earlier I mentioned that Elijah was on a roller-coaster going from the height of excitement to the depths of despair. The people of Judah rode a similar roller coaster as they rebuilt the wall. They still had their enemies mocking them, the work was hard, and they got tired. They had to make adjustments, such as only having half the men work while the other half stood guard.[27] However, with a sure, focused leader and lots of encouragement, the people learned not to give into fear but to trust God to protect them.

Am I giving in to fear or allowing God to protect me?

> *"Let me describe the one who truly follows me and does what I say. He is like a man who chooses the right place to build a house and then lays a deep and secure foundation. When the storms and floods rage against that house, it continues to stand strong and unshaken through the tempest, for it has been wisely built on the right foundation."* [28]

We keep fear and insecurity away as we focus on God and build our walls His way. Not only is the protective wall formed, but the foundation on which we stand becomes firm.

I mentioned before that I had served on the pastoral staff at a church for over thirteen years. I knew that my time on staff there was coming to an end; I could feel it in my spirit but was waiting for the right timing. As I was driving home one day, the Holy Spirit filled the car and the *whisper*, that *still small voice* said, "It's time." At that very moment, all the concern about the timing disappeared as peace filled me to the very core of my being.

As I began the journey of resigning and telling the congregation, I remember one well-meaning individual coming up to me. They began sharing stories of people who had stepped out in faith and failed. I quickly realized that the demonic was trying to find a weak spot for fear and insecurity to creep in. I wasn't just taking a step forward with God, I was taking a huge leap. There was no back-up plan or Plan B if I failed. It was full forward.

At that moment, I had to make a choice. Was I going to trust God and take the risk? Was I going to allow fear of failure rule the day? Was I going to let all the negative reasons from a worldly perspective come rampaging in? Or, was I going to stay the course?

That day I made a very conscious decision to block out the fear and insecurity that was knocking at the door. Believe me, they knocked and sometimes pounded loudly on the door. They were uninvited guests and I was determined not to allow them into my mind or spirit. I had recorded the words people had given me from the Lord. I had the messages that God had given me directly, along with my dreams and visions. I had allowed God's dream to marinate for many years and trusted Him to be faithful with the timing. It was one of those moments when I knew, because I knew, because I knew it was time. I realized that I could not allow my mind to entertain fear or insecurity for even one moment. I would read my journal and worship, which effectively not only shut the door, but nailed that door shut. Lies, fears and insecurity were not allowed to enter!

There will always be opportunities for fear and insecurity to hop back in. However, I would suggest that God gives us more opportunities to reinforce the wall. As I write this, I think back on all the dreams, visions, and words that God gave directly to me. I also remember the prophetic words that were spoken over and over before I made the giant leap. God, in His gracious love, had also given me additional dreams, words and prophetic words that acted like jet fuel to keep me moving forward. He opened doors that I never imagined, and I know there are still more to come. However, I have realized that I must keep my focus because, like Elijah, it only takes a moment, or one person, to throw me off track.

There is only true freedom when I rest in who God is. The wonderful thing about our God is that He is alive. He is not made from stone or a fantasy. He is alive, active and interested in me. When I understood that He truly loved me and wanted what is best for me, I found peace. Another way to say this is that I learned to rest in His presence.

Fear and insecurity do not have any home or entry point when we rest in the peace and presence of God.

SPIRITUAL MUSCLE BUILDING

QUESTIONS

1. On a scale of 0-10, rate your level of fear and insecurity (0 being none – 10 being very high).

2. What is keeping you from leaving fear and insecurity behind and grabbing onto God's outstretched hand?

ACTION STEPS

1. Confess and repent of anything that is holding you back from experiencing the peace that God has to offer.

2. Take a few moments and write down where you have seen God work in your life and thank Him for each time.

3. Take time to worship. Worship chases away fear and insecurity.

PRAYER AND DECLARATION

Heavenly Father, I ask that You bring to light every entry point for fear and insecurity. I commit to surrender those areas to You and I invite You to bring healing into the very core of my being. Where fear and insecurity have invaded my mind, I speak peace. I acknowledge that fear has no place in my life because You are my strong tower, the place of refuge and the One I can run to and hide.

I decree and declare that I am a child of God and that fear has no place within me. I decree and declare that my footing is secure with Jesus Christ as my foundation and cornerstone. I declare that I will not worry about tomorrow but trust in Your faithfulness. Your lovingkindness towards me never runs out. I decree and declare that I will lean back into Jesus and live from a place of peace, knowing that You are faithful. You have my life in the very palm of Your hands. Thank you, Lord, for peace that surpasses understanding and Your joy that fills my heart.

SCRIPTURAL BASIS:

Matthew 6:34, Psalm 34:4, Psalm 94:19, Lamentations 3:22-23

CHAPTER FIVE

UNLOCKING THE BALL AND CHAIN

"...nine out of ten people I have had to forgive sincerely do not feel they have done anything wrong. It is up to me to forgive them from my heart—and then keep quiet about it."[1]

R.T. KENDALL

UNFORGIV'EN, adjective Not forgiven; not pardoned.[2]

FORGIV'ENESS, *noun* forgiv'ness.[3]

1. The act of forgiving; the pardon of an offender, by which he is considered and treated as not guilty. The *forgiveness* of enemies is a Christian duty.

2. The pardon or remission of an offense or crime; as the *forgiveness* of sin or of injuries.

Ruth's Short Version: Forgiveness removes the chains of bondage that real or perceived actions or words have placed on me. Forgiveness allows me to truly experience life as God intended it to be, both in relationship to others and to Him.

PRAYER

Heavenly Father, please reveal any areas where unforgiveness has a foothold in my life. It is my desire to do forgiveness Your way, rather than the world's way. I ask that you position me for breakthrough. In Jesus' name, Amen.

Practically speaking, forgiveness is not an easy thing. When I was in school, we were always told that we could not use a word to define a word. However, you'll see in the definition above they did just that. Remarkably, forgiveness is a word that means different things to different people.

Growing up, I was taught that you had only genuinely forgiven if you had also forgotten about the offense. This put me in a quandary as there were offenses that I certainly couldn't forget. Learning what forgiveness truly was, and was not, brought clarification and freedom into my life, allowing God to strategically position me in ways that I never imagined.

When I first began to study the topic of forgiveness, I found the majority of teachings were from a slanted perspective that didn't cover the full scope of the topic. Fortunately, much has changed. We have come to understand that there is tremendous power in forgiveness; but for some, forgiveness is one of the hardest things they will ever do.

COUNTERFEIT VS. REAL

When I was in my late teens and early twenties, I worked as a teller in several banks. For each bank, I had to successfully complete their teller training course. Throughout the process of the training, we had to learn how to properly handle all aspects of the job requirements from depositing money to cashing checks, from opening a drawer to balancing out at night. Of course, there was also the vault, the alarm system, how to survive an audit, and how to handle a robbery. To top it off, we had to learn to spot counterfeit money.

In the 1980's, we didn't have special markers or machines to discern the counterfeit from the real. We had to learn to tell the difference by sight and touch. And the way to learn the difference was to handle the real thing. The more we dealt with the real currency, the less likely we would be fooled by the counterfeit. When handling money, the counterfeit just didn't feel right. In other words, the tellers had to be so familiar with the real that they knew something was off.

This is the same with Scripture. The more we take time to get into the Word, the more likely it is that we will realize when something is off or counterfeit.

I share this story because the more we understand what forgiveness looks and feels like, the less likely we will become trapped in the arena of unforgiveness. The more we know the Word of God, the more we will recognize the truth. The more we spend time with God in conversation, the more we will know His voice. When we know the Author (God) and we know His Word (the Bible), we will quickly learn to recognize the counterfeit. It may be just a gut feeling that something is off. Or, it may be a huge warning bell going off in our minds that something doesn't align with Scripture. Whether we can fully put our finger on the issue or not, we will know that something is wrong.

COLORFUL GARMENTS, COLORFUL FAMILIES

In Genesis 37, we have the story of Joseph and his coat of many colors. A coat has numerous functions, but ultimately, it is a covering. In Joseph's family, I am sure all the boys had coats that were culturally acceptable. As in each family, every child has a unique personality, and each child is created to be valued. We are told in Scripture that Joseph's father made a very special coat for Joseph. The problem arose because Joseph's coat was different from his brothers' which naturally set him apart from them.

Favoritism can be real or perceived. But remember, even perceived bias feels authentic to the individual involved! Every child is asking if they are valued or loved. When one child is favored, the other siblings feel undervalued or unloved. Not only was Joseph the favored child with a special, colorful coat, he was also a dreamer. Today, we would say that his head was always in the clouds. All of this and more became a breeding ground for anger, resentment, and unforgiveness within his brothers.

Joseph likely bragged about his colorful coat, shared his dreams and quite possibly taunted his brothers about being the favored child. Remember, he was human and, truthfully, all of us want to be the favored child. I cannot tell you how often I have heard my kids say, "I'm the favorite." We're good as long as they all believe that! However, when we don't feel favored, we feel less than everyone else. Feeling undervalued or overlooked can open the door for multiple issues to come storming in without our realizing it. One issue that comes in with a vengeance is unforgiveness.

We make assumptions that some people can forgive more easily than others because they had some sort of fantastic upbringing. However, that's not always the case. Let's look at Joseph's early life in a nutshell.

Joseph's father was a man named Jacob. Jacob had deceived his own brother by stealing his birthright and shortly thereafter even deceived his father into thinking he was his brother, Esau. Jacob ends up leaving his family home to search for a wife. He meets a woman by the name of Rachel and falls deeply in love with her. Before they can marry, he has to negotiate with her father. Jacob had to work for his future father-in-law for the next seven years to secure his bride. The joyous wedding celebration happens and the next morning Jacob discovers that he is not married to his beloved Rachel but rather to her sister Leah.

Jacob, who had deceived his own family, is now deceived by his father-in-law. He confronts his father-in-law and wedding number two is negotiated. He had to work for another seven years to pay for the bride he wanted in the first place. Now, let me point out that Jacob is now married to sisters. That's a story all in itself!

Jacob, Leah and Rachel lived within a culture where women were shamed if they were unable to bear a child. Leah gives Jacob several children; however, Rachel is barren. Jealousy explodes within the family and Jacob ends up sleeping with Rachel's maid and, eventually, with Leah's maid, producing children with them both. Finally, Joseph is born to Rachel. Look at the family dynamics. The family is riddled with deception. In addition, the family unit is full of step-mothers, step-brothers, and a step-sister all vying for the love and attention of one man, Jacob.

As we allow God to strategically position us, it is important to realize that we tend to walk out what was modeled within our family. This can be a conscious or subconscious decision, but it is a decision nonetheless. We need to ask God to show us the things that we believe and do just because they are part of our family's behavior and belief patterns.

As Joseph flaunted his colorful coat, I'm sure it was a combination of being one of the youngest children and showing off that he was Daddy's (Jacob's) favorite. As his brothers' rage and jealousy increased, they behaved in a way that was been modeled by their family with more deception and jealousy.

Decisions made in a moment of anger can have a lasting impact on the family, on others, and on generations to come. The brothers' deception and jealousy became so strong that they devised a plan to eliminate Joseph from the family. I cannot imagine the extent of family dysfunction that leads a whole group of brothers to agree to throw Joseph into a pit, and, ultimately, sell him into slavery. I also cannot imagine what Joseph went through as he was thrown into the pit, then hauled out of the pit, sold into slavery, dragged away, and forced into slavery in a foreign land. All this happened as this young man tried to process that his brothers were responsible for his suffering.

Bill Johnson, senior pastor at Bethel Church in Redding, California, makes a great statement. "What you know about God changes who you are. It defines your purpose. It defines your destiny. It shapes how you think most of all. Everything comes from your perspective on life."[4]

Amid Joseph's massively dysfunctional family, I have to wonder what he learned about God that drew him toward rather than push him away from God. Part of Joseph's culture included passing down stories of God's faithfulness. A good Jewish family would tell and retell these stories. Joseph may well have remembered the stories of his forefathers and the faithfulness of God as he journeyed from the pit, to prison, and eventually, to the palace.

What stories am I telling myself to remind me of God's faithfulness?

In the midst of my suffering, what am I learning about God? Am I drawing closer to or pulling away from God in my situation? What about you?

Look again at Stephen when he was being stoned. With his very last breath, he SHOUTED a prayer that went through the atmosphere to the very gates of heaven.

> "He crumpled to his knees and shouted in a loud voice, 'Our Lord, don't hold this sin against them.' And then he died." [5]

At this moment, several things were happening. Again, put yourself in Stephen's place. He was physically being stoned, his body beaten, torn, bruised and broken. Stephen knew that he was going to die. During these final moments on earth, he had a choice to make. We could say that he had every right to be angry with the mob gathered around him. He had every right to be angry with those people taunting and throwing the stones. However, with a voice racked with pain as he was taking his final breath, he cared for the people around him.

Stephen was able to see past his own physical pain and look out for the eternal destiny of every person there. Stephen himself refused to be bound by unforgiveness as He pleaded with God not to charge them with his death. But let's take it one step further. He modeled what a relationship with Father God looked like. He poured out love and forgiveness in the midst of pain and suffering just as Jesus did on the cross when He died for our sins. He saw beyond the moment with the Father's eyes.

> *"Under Roman law, Stephen's death was illegal. The Sanhedrin was not authorized to impose the death penalty, but the stoning appeared to be the result of mob action. There is no mention in Acts of anyone being punished for the death of Stephen."* [6]

Go back to the story of Stephen. Stoning was not uncommon, so the crowd had seen and maybe even participated in this type of death before. Yet Stephen was different. There was no anger and no revenge. There was only forgiveness. Stephen positioned himself to walk in forgiveness and by doing this, he was ultimately positioning those stoning him to have an opportunity to experience forgiveness. Think about that. How do we respond when we are wronged? Can we look up to heaven and ask that the sin not be held against them and loose them through forgiveness?

One of the many things that challenges the whole concept of forgiveness is when we are unjustly accused. I had a situation at work where I was falsely accused, and it has been one of the more difficult things for me to work through. I am a person who values integrity and a false accusation hits pretty hard.

When we finally had a staff discussion about what had happened, the person who had made the accusation admitted that they had made assumptions and should have asked more questions. However, my punishment for the perceived wrong was never pulled back, nor was the same requirement extended to the rest of the employees. Was I justified in my feelings? Sure. Was I right to hold onto the wrong done against me? No. That was not healthy, and as long as I held onto it, I allowed it to have power over me. Yes, I was wronged, but I had to choose whether I wanted to be free or be held captive.

Sometimes, we can be slammed so hard that we need to work through our emotions in a safe manner. The first thing I did was clean my office. I figured either I'd have a very clean office to use, or it would be easier to pack up and leave. As I worked on my office, seething with frustration and anger, one of my peers asked me to promise that I would not resign in anger. They realized that I had reached my tipping point. They also knew that I never wanted to resign in anger but always in blessing. Good grief. I taught on this stuff!

As I mentioned, although a conversation took place, the punishment was never pulled back. Therefore, I had a constant reminder of the conflict which remained unresolved for me. When we feel forced to live with an unresolved situation with no visible solution, it becomes very difficult to forgive because it is always in our face. I made a conscious choice to forgive and I made that choice over and over again until it began to take root. I decided to pray for blessings over those who were involved every time I thought about the situation. Granted, for some time I forced myself to do this, but my feelings caught up eventually. I actually remained in that position for another year before I resigned, in God's timing and with His blessing.

Let me encourage you. Never let pain and unforgiveness win. Child of God, with His help you can forgive and be free.

PAIN TO GREATNESS

I think we can all relate to a deep wound received from a friend. The only way we can ever develop deep friendships is to take the risk. However, things happen, and pain enters.

> *"Faithful are the wounds of a friend [who corrects out of love and concern], But the kisses of an enemy are deceitful [because they serve his hidden agenda]."* [7]

Through no fault of my own, I found myself stuck in the middle of a very sticky situation. My best friend had lost her position, and I had been asked to step into it. I wrestled with the Lord. Just for the record, I never applied for the job; they sought me out. I still remember the night they approached me to come on staff. To be honest, I was angry. I wasn't mad at my friend, nor at the organization; I was angry at God. Why? Because I knew that being obedient would cost me that friendship. Sure enough, at that point in time, we couldn't make it past the issues that both of us carried in the transition, and my friend and I went our separate ways.

Many people feel that they cannot get angry at God. Granted, we can argue that unforgiveness and anger are two different things, especially since God is perfect in all His ways.[8] However, God is not only God, He is also our Friend. I can get angry at my earthly friends, so I can get angry at my heavenly Father, too. Carrying anger toward God or denying it is there becomes another area of bondage, just like unforgiveness.

When we are angry with God, the best thing we can do is admit it. We so often try to hide it because we know that He is perfect. As a parent, we can be totally right in something we are telling our child, and yet they may still throw a temper-tantrum and sulk for a bit. As parents, we still love them and want to help them work through it. I see Father God watching us throw our temper-tantrum when we don't agree with or understand what He is doing. Yet, He loves us all the same, knows what we are going through, and longs to walk us through it.

I quickly learned that the first question I needed to ask myself was whether or not my walk with God was more important than the friendship. Following that, I needed to allow my friend to feel and process what was happening, and I needed to do the same. I had to relinquish the infamous "why" question to God and trust that He truly was in control of the bigger picture. I could admit to Him that I was angry and ask Him to forgive me in the midst of that. And, I made a choice to trust Him.

Due to confidentiality, neither my friend nor I were able to share all the components of the story. People pushed me for reconciliation and I imagine my friend was also pushed for the same. Neither of us handled the situation one hundred percent correctly; we were both wounded. We didn't hate each other, but the friendship couldn't survive the twists and turns that our lives were taking.

During this situation, Jack Frost, from Shiloh Place Ministries, came to do a weekend conference. It was all about reconciliation. I was less than excited about being there, but I was on staff, so I put on my game face and attended. God knew the dread in my heart. I was in the foyer when Jack came up to me and began to talk privately to me about what was happening. To this day, I don't know if our senior pastor clued him in or if it was Holy Spirit. Most likely it was a combination of both.

Jack shared about shifts in relationships when God calls one or both people into a different level of ministry. I had to learn that reconciliation is built on trust, and takes two, whereas forgiveness only takes one. He shared with me that transitions bring new friends and relationships into our lives, even while we let other ones go. If we cannot navigate those shifts, we will never be able to walk into all that God has for us.

That conversation began to set me free. I realized that I needed to work through my issues. When I thought of those involved, I began to ask the Lord to bless them abundantly, asking God to open doors for them beyond my wildest expectations. I could forgive all those involved and myself, even if the relationship with my friend was never reconciled. I had to learn that reconciliation is not a measure of forgiveness.

I like to use illustrations when I speak. For those who are visual learners, a well thought out prop can make all the difference. Our dog had one of those giant balls with a rope through it. Its purpose was to play tug of war with the dog. When relating to our topic, the arena of forgiveness vs. unforgiveness creates a tug of war that can go to the very core of our being.

Visualize an old-fashioned tug of war rope with the mud pit in the middle. One side consists of unforgiveness with its counterparts of anger, resentment, revenge, etc. The other side is forgiveness with its counterparts of peace, security, joy, etc. Which side is going to land on their bottoms in the mud pit? If forgiveness lands in the mud, we ceased to take ground and have become covered with grime. However, if forgiveness wins and pulls the unforgiveness into the mud pit, the mud actually becomes springs of living water to cleanse us and set us free to soar.

We can never go wrong when we side with forgiveness. And, be assured that when the situation is too difficult to forgive, we can ask God to help us get to the point where we are even willing to forgive. Even that prayer has powerful impact that will keep us from landing in the mud. Remember, Jesus died on the cross so our sins could be forgiven. He knows what pain and humiliation feel like. He knows the journey and is more than able to help our feelings catch up to a decision to forgive. He's got this; and He's got you.

I love that Peter, with his usual boldness, was the one that asked Jesus the well-known question, *"Lord, how often should I forgive someone who sins against me? Seven times?"*[9] There is an important key to remember. When we stop short of the fullness of forgiveness, we remain in bondage and never excel to the greatness that God intended for us. Jesus fully understood this as He responded, *"'No, not seven times,' Jesus replied, 'but seventy times seven!'"*[10]

I can hear some of your brains already doing the math. In our humanness, we love to keep a tally of wrongs, real and perceived, that people have done to us. However, God's desire is that we just keep on forgiving. When Peter asked this question, he was most likely relying on the tradition of the times. The Jewish rabbi's taught that you only needed to forgive three times.[11] So, in Peter's mind, he probably thought his question was full of overwhelming generosity.

Over the years, I have spoken with many people who have been in complicated situations who have wanted to know how much longer they have to walk in forgiveness. Human standards can be very different than God's standards. It's always best to align with God, even when we don't understand.

"But instead be kind and affectionate toward one another. Has God graciously forgiven you? Then graciously forgive one another in the depths of Christ's love." [12]

Back to my teaching prop—the dog toy. I removed the rope, painted the ball black and ran a chain through the hole in the ball. You guessed it, a ball and chain. Walking in unforgiveness becomes an invisible cage or ball and chain that confines us and impacts us physically, emotionally and spiritually.

Taking on the offense is like putting ourselves in a cage or fastening a ball and chain around our ankle. There is a transaction that occurs. In the spiritual realm, the one offended is thrown the key. Many of us remain locked in our cage or drag around our personal ball and chain because we don't realize that as followers of Jesus, we also hold the key that can set us free.

Too often, we are waiting for the one who offended us to ask for forgiveness, and to take responsibility for their actions. Granted, that would be nice. However, as Corrie Ten Boom said, *"Forgiveness is an act of the will, and the will can function regardless of the temperature of the heart."* [13] Even if they do apologize, we ultimately discover that the person who wronged us doesn't hold the key to our freedom after all. Unless we forgive, we are still in as much bondage as we were before.

Many people, like Corrie Ten Boom, experienced horrific events as they walked through life. In and of themselves, they don't have the ability to forgive. It is essential to understand that forgiveness is often a process and doesn't always come quickly. How often have we heard the old clichés, "Just get over it" or "Forgive and forget"? To recognize that we have the key doesn't mean that we have the strength to take the key, put it in the lock, and turn it. Sometimes, we get the key in the lock and it gets stuck as we struggle with the feelings and emotions which may surround the issue. I cannot count the number of times I have asked someone if they are willing to ask the Lord to help them begin the process of forgiving.

PROCESS TOWARD FREEDOM

Is forgiveness a process? Yes. Forgiveness doesn't happen overnight. It takes constant reliance upon God. Especially if the individual keeps offending us, or we find ourselves frequently in positions where we are falsely accused, falsely imprisoned, or forgotten. The good news is that we have an amazing God who honors our decision to forgive and will help our feelings and emotions to catch up with that decision. That reminds me again of Joseph.

Joseph was seventeen years old when he was sold into slavery. When I was seventeen, I graduated from high school and was heading off to college. I guess you could say that, in my mind, life was just beginning. At that young age, Joseph's life was going through a significant overhaul that he could not understand. Joseph experienced his life; he didn't just read about it. He had to walk through it without knowing the outcome. As Joseph walked through life, he was unknowingly being strategically positioned for more than he could ever ask or imagine.

When we read Scripture, we forget that these stories are about people just like us with hopes and dreams. As we read the account of Joseph, we know that everything worked out in the end. However, we need to take a step back and realize that Joseph didn't know God's plan for him or his family. Fear and insecurity were undoubtedly knocking at his door. Hatred and bitterness were lurking as the caravan moved toward Egypt. All Joseph could do was hang on. He was in for many challenges and transitions that would ultimately move him from pain into greatness.

Am I willing to forgive so I can walk into the fullness of my destiny? Or am I going to hang onto the wounding and forfeit the plans that God has for me?

> *"'For I know the plans I have for you,' says the Lord. 'They are plans for good and not for disaster, to give you a future and a hope. In those days when you pray, I will listen. If you look for me wholeheartedly, you will find me. I will be found by you,' says the Lord. 'I will end your captivity and restore your fortunes. I will gather you out of the nations where I sent you and will bring you home again to your own land.'"* [14]

Joseph endured being sold by his brothers, taken into captivity to a strange land, imprisoned, falsely accused, rejected, and forgotten. As he wrestled through all of the human thoughts and feelings that went with his experience, there was something very different about him. He held every thought captive. He made a conscious decision to not allow unforgiveness hold him captive. Joseph watched where his thoughts wandered. He controlled them; they did not control him. As Joseph held his thoughts captive, he allowed God to work in and through him.

Eventually, Joseph is placed in a position of power, second only to Pharaoh. From this position, he saved the nation of Egypt. However, that is not the end of the story. Joseph showed his brothers he was able to respond from a heavenly perspective, rather than from a place of pain. He also saved his own people from starvation. Joseph fully recognized that God had woven everything together. There was no hidden cage for Joseph or his family; there was only undying love, freedom and reconciliation.

The accounts of Joseph and Stephen mentioned in this chapter are vastly different. However, the common denominator is that both learned to forgive. Because they were able to freely forgive, they were strategically positioned for lasting impact upon the Kingdom of God, impact that continues to echo throughout the ages. Neither of them allowed themselves to be caged or chained by unforgiveness. Rather, they walked hand in hand with God as they practiced amazing levels of forgiveness.

SPIRITUAL MUSCLE BUILDING

QUESTIONS

What do I believe about forgiveness?

How is my belief system demonstrated in my every day activities?

ACTION STEPS

Make a conscious choice to forgive anyone who has offended you. Remember, you hold the key to set yourself free because of what Jesus did on the Cross.

Ask the Lord to help you forgive and allow your feelings to catch up to your conscious decision.

Determine not to take back anything that is not of God. Pray blessing over the individual(s) who have wounded you.

Take time to worship and thank God for His mercy, grace and forgiveness.

PRAYER AND DECLARATION

Heavenly Father, when Jesus was dying on the Cross, He cried out for You to forgive everyone who took part in His death. He paid for every sin that I would ever commit, covered all my guilt and condemnation, and bore them all on the Cross. He rose victorious over it all. I thank You that I am created in Your image. Therefore, as I lean into You, I can truly forgive. You have done so much for me and have forgiven me of so much. I ask You to help me forgive others and even myself. I don't want to be held in bondage. It is my desire to soar with You.

Heavenly Father, Your Word says that I can soar on the wings of eagles. There is such freedom in that statement. I declare that I am free to experience life. I declare that I am filled with the joy of the Lord. I declare that I will be a vessel of grace and forgiveness as I imitate You. I thank You that I carry blessing, not cursing, and that my blessings will be multiplied. I thank You that since You are victorious, I can also walk in victory. I declare that I am free because of You.

SCRIPTURAL BASIS:
Isaiah 40:32, Galatians 5:22-23, Ephesians 5:1,
Proverbs 11:25, John 10:10

CHAPTER SIX

GRAVEYARD TO GARDEN

"Come hell or high water you will never take me back to the place I was before. I have been through too much to let life whoop me again. My faith is stronger than it's ever been, my mind is more tenacious than it's ever been, my soul is more absolute."[1]

T.D. JAKES

TRAU·MA, noun ˈtrȯ-mə *also* ˈtrau̇-ma[2]

1 b: a disordered psychic or behavioral state resulting from severe mental or emotional stress or physical injury.

c: an emotional upset.

2 an agent, force, or mechanism that causes trauma.

Ruth's Version: Trauma is different for everyone. What is traumatic to one person isn't necessarily traumatic to another. In other words, we need to listen as people share their stories and not assume that what is trauma to us, is trauma to them, and vice-versa. We have a fantastic military. They can fight the same battle and have the same experience yet each soldier will process the events differently. One will come back with PTSD (Post Traumatic Stress Disorder) while another will not. Another example would be the individual who survives a severe automobile accident and struggles to even get in a car, while another person, who experienced the same severity of an accident, is seemingly unscathed. For another, it may be the loss of a loved one, a job, or a natural disaster. The list goes on and on.

As you read through this section, my desire is that we all are reminded that there is help for those suffering from a traumatic experience. We should not judge another's experience based on our own experience. Just minister healing to the hurting. We serve a God who heals, redeems, restores and wants to turn our graveyards into gardens for His glory.

BLINDSIDED BUT NOT DESTROYED

Some seasons in life manage to turn your life upside down and inside out. 2014 was one of those years for our family. We entered the year with my brother-in-law, David, battling cancer. He loved the Lord and was part of a church that believed in healing. The elders had prayed and prayed for him and David was holding firmly onto the Lord. However, one day he called and shared a dream with us. In his dream, he saw his father and brother (both deceased) standing in a field. As the dream unfolded, his impression was "Not yet, but soon, he would join them."

It wasn't long before he shared another dream. David had a very dry sense of humor and God often speaks to us in ways that are unique to our personalities. At this point, David had some huge tumors that were quite visible. In the dream, there was an old man with a vegetable peeler. He was peeling away the tumors. When David questioned him about it, the man said, "Sonny, you don't need these anymore." David shared with us that he knew he would soon be transitioning from this world to heaven and that the tumors were not going along. The interesting thing was, he was at total peace. As the dream had unfolded, God had given him the meaning and David was resolute. He had met with God and in the process, had been given grace to die in peace.

June rolled around, and David called to say good-bye. We knew that we needed to get back to see him. However, the week we were to go, our youngest daughter was thrown from a horse and had a concussion, so we delayed the trip by a week. David was still talking to us over the phone and doing seemingly well so we were not overly concerned about a delay. The following weekend, we made the seven-hour drive expecting to see him that evening. However, there was a severe accident on the highway, which caused another delay and a detour. Since we didn't get into town until after 10pm, we decided to get some sleep and see him in the morning. At 3am, my phone rang. It was the expected but dreaded phone call.

In the middle of any death or trauma, one important aspect we must recognize is that God is moving. Just as He had overwhelmed David with His love as his days on this earth wound to a close, He was also watching over the family. In a season of grief or trauma, a challenge for all of us is to intentionally look for God's hand in its midst. In this case, we arrived at hospice at the same moment as my mother-in-law, Maxine, drove up.

Maxine was saying goodbye and burying the second of her four children. She had also buried her husband. The grief and guilt were massive as we walked into the room. David had died alone by his own choice. He had chosen not to let the family know how quickly his body was shutting down. Of course, none of us would have chosen that route for him. We would have been there, hence guilt walked in. As that guilt knocked at the door, we also had to acknowledge that only God could orchestrate each of our arrivals at the exact moment, so we could walk in together and no one was alone.

David's memorial service was the next weekend. Our entire family again made the seven-hour drive to be there. I vividly remember standing outside the funeral home just minutes before the service started when my phone rang. That call would shake our family even more.

Our youngest daughter was working her way into the professional horse arena. Working at this level is more than a hobby and different than a job. You invest time, energy, resources (including financial resources), and you own a horse with a future. This type of horse and rider connection is also very different from owning a dog or a cat. At only eighteen, she had already been working in the industry for about five years. The best analogy would be an apprenticeship program, where the student lives and works with their "master" as they learn a trade, eventually becoming a master craftsman themselves. In other words, she was fully immersed in the industry.

As I looked at the phone, I saw that it was her trainer calling. I answered the phone to learn that Donna's beloved horse had died unexpectedly and tragically. I was about to walk into my brother-in-law's funeral knowing that as soon as it was over, we had to tell our daughter that her world was caving in. Some people would later make callous comments such as: "She'll get over it," and, "It's just an animal." But this was so much more, it was the shattering of a future filled with hopes, dreams, and deep love of a creature. All this was happening right at a pivotal moment in her life as death and trauma came stampeding through to shatter her world.

As parents, our hearts were broken. We were already grieving Mark's brother. We were supporting his mom. And now we had the situation with our daughter. I must step back at this point and say that our other four kids were great in that moment. It brings tears to my eyes thinking about it even now. They looked at me and said, "Mom, you have to take care of Dad and Grandma...we've got Donna". They loaded her in the car and headed for home while Mark and I swallowed hard and managed to get through the day.

That night, Mark and I went for a walk and just cried. We cried for his mom and the weight of sorrow that had enveloped her as she buried another child. We cried for Donna and the pain that she was feeling. We felt so helpless in that moment. We could not clone ourselves and be everyplace we needed to be; we had no answers, only questions. Our hearts were breaking.

On the home front, our daughter, Donna, also had more questions than anyone had answers. At just eighteen, the weight of anger and grief was crushing. Focus, direction, excitement and her planned future were ripped away. Our hearts would continue to break as we watched her struggle for the next four years, trying to find her future and regain her destiny again.

Through David's death, and the situation revolving around Donna, it was easy to ask God the *why* question. I'm sure we can all relate to that. We want to demand answers from God for the pain that we experience in our lives. We want Him to justify everything. After all, He is almighty and powerful. If He is truly in control, then how can our lives be altered so drastically in one moment of time?

> The truth is that He is God. He sees the whole picture and not just a part, and He is faithful. So, when we demand an answer to the *Why, God?* question, we are demanding to judge whether His actions are fair in our sight.

Unfortunately, the year wasn't over yet. Within a month, we found out that Mark's mom had pancreatic cancer. Physically, they didn't feel that surgery was an option, and she didn't really want to live either. We entered a time of trying to support Donna at home, helping her process, while running back and forth to care for Maxine, who was a seven-hour drive away. In November, the family gathered yet again as we said a very tearful goodbye to Maxine.

RAGS TO RICHES

As I mentioned before, trauma is as unique as the individual who experiences it. In the Bible there is the story of a woman named Esther. Her story is comparable to the Cinderella story—a rags-to-riches story, for sure. With both the fairy tale story of Cinderella, and the biblical account of Esther, we tend to look at the ending and declare, "They all lived happily ever after." What we miss, in that short-sighted viewpoint, is the journey, the pain, the trauma, and *then* the triumph.

Esther (her Persian name) was also known as Hadassah (Jewish name). Scripture also tells us she was an orphan growing up in a foreign country and being raised by her cousin, Mordecai, because her parents were deceased. The story tells us that the Persian king struggled with both drinking and anger. During a drunken feast, the queen was forever banished from King Xerxes' presence. Playing out like a Broadway play, the scene continues to unfold as the king comes to his senses and realizes what he has done. Swiftly, his personal attendants come in to make their suggestions.

> *"Let us search the empire to find beautiful young virgins for the king."* [3]

We live in a world where sex trafficking is a huge industry. Our hearts ache for those who have been caught up in it. With that in mind, consider how Esther felt as she was chosen (taken).

> *"So his personal attendants suggested, 'Let us search the empire to bring these beautiful young women into the royal harem at the fortress of Susa.' Because of the king's decree, Esther, along with many other young women, was brought to the king's harem."* [4]

No doubt, the town gossip centered around the king, the banishment of the queen, and his decree. As these young girls were led away, I am sure that fear and terror ran rampant. They were forcibly taken away from their families and the life they knew. They were put into a highly controlled environment. Their own futures, as well as their hopes and dreams, had all come to a crashing halt.

Although the palace seems like a fantastic place in fairy tales, put yourself in the position of a young girl being hauled away, knowing that she'd soon be *sleeping* with the king, and would most likely be rejected and perhaps killed. And, what if she *is* the one that he chooses? Would she fall under the same condemnation as her predecessor?

One of the things that amazes me about Esther is that we don't have a record of her ever complaining. We cannot make the mistake of thinking that what she experienced was easy. Instead, she leaned in for wisdom to make it through. She was willing to learn, even during a difficult situation. And because of that steadfast heart, God used her to save her entire nation.

In the midst of our graveyard, in the midst of our trauma, God is always faithful to develop a beautiful garden. However, it is difficult to see clearly through the moments of pain and sorrow.

The question is: Are we able to trust that God is moving in and through the bigger picture in ways that we may not understand? In a season of trauma, we can easily lose our ability to dream. We must often make a conscious choice to trust the God of the universe is still planting seeds in our garden that will be beautiful in His timing.

As I write this, I see a garden with God as the gardener, lovingly and patiently tending what He has planted. When we keep our focus on the Lord, our garden will not be destroyed. The seeds are being watered with tears. Even through the pain, it will be watered and it will grow in due time. If you have lost your ability to dream, ask the Lord to help you dream again.

COMPLAINING VS. CONVERSATION

Have you ever been in a relationship with someone who is always negative, untrusting and a complainer? They may always see the cup as half empty rather than half full, or they only see the cloud rather than the silver lining?

Complaining can easily become a trap that keeps us from experiencing the fullness of comfort and healing that God loves to pour out on His children.

Throughout my years in ministry, I have been in relationships with people who are complainers. To be blunt, they would drain all my energy and I wanted to run away. I think we all fall into that category at times. However, I am so thankful that God's response is very different from mine. God has the ever-listening and patient ear that is always turned toward us. However, a relationship is not one-sided. An authentic relationship only comes through conversation between the parties involved.

As any parent knows, every child is different and has a unique personality filled with likes and dislikes. For example, let's look at Cain and Abel, two of Adam and Eve's children.

> *"When they grew up, Abel became a shepherd, while Cain cultivated the ground. When it was time for the harvest, Cain presented some of his crops as a gift to the Lord. Abel also brought a gift—the best portions of the firstborn lambs from his flock. The Lord accepted Abel and his gift, but He did not accept Cain and his gift. This made Cain very angry, and he looked dejected. 'Why are you so angry?' the Lord asked Cain. 'Why do you look so dejected? You will be accepted if you do what is right. But if you refuse to do what is right, then watch out! Sin is crouching at the door, eager to control you. But you must subdue it and be its master.'"* [5]

On the surface, we wonder why God didn't accept Cain's offering. Wesley gives some vital insight into the situation. "*But the great difference was, Abel offered in faith, and Cain did not. Abel offered with an eye to God's will as his rule, and in dependence upon the promise of a Redeemer. But Cain did not offer in faith, and so it turned into sin to him.*"[6] It is important, in our walk with Christ that we look to Him in faith. It is never our works that get us into heaven. Abel offered his *best* while Cain just offered *some*.

Ask yourself this question. Am I offering my best to God, or am I only offering some?

Cain's heart was not in the right place. He was meeting an obligation rather than entering a relationship. As Cain became dejected, he entered a mindset of entitlement and complaining, rather than conversation with God and a heart set on love. God always desires relationship and He met Cain right where he was and invited him into a conversation.

I find it interesting that during this conversation, God gave Cain a promise and a warning. The promise was that: "*You will be accepted if you do what is right.*"[7]

How we handle these moments will radically impact the outcome of our lives. We can be assured that when we make mistakes, or when we experience trauma, God will also make things right. It may look different than we think it should, but He promises to be there. However, we must invite Him into the situation and learn to see things through His perspective. God also gave Cain a stern warning: "*But if you refuse to do what is right, then watch out! Sin is crouching at the door, eager to control you.*"[8]

As we walked through 2014, there were many things that did not line up with our perfect depiction of life. I would often think of Psalm 23. God tells us that we walk through the valley of the shadow of death. The words *walk through* tell me that we are not meant to camp there.

We cannot stay in the place of grief but must make a choice to trust that God ultimately watches over the outcome even if we cannot see it in the moment. Traumatic experiences can open the door to the sin that is crouching at the door, eager to pull us away from God and control us. Cain chose to allow his situation to pull him away from God rather than to draw him closer. He chose resentment and complaining, rather than conversation and relationship.

Remember, the biblical accounts that we read are about real people in real situations. Most people know the story of Job.[9] Job lost everything except his wife. He could only sit by, helplessly, as his children, livestock and material possessions were destroyed. As Job journeys through the trauma and the grief, he certainly complains.[10] However, he makes a telling statement, one that is vital for us to grasp in our lives.

> *"At least I can take comfort in this: Despite the pain, I have not denied the words of the Holy One."* [11]

In the midst of the pain, Job never denied God's faithfulness. But that doesn't mean that he didn't pour out his pain—pain that eventually became unbearable. Job realized that the only place he could turn was to God because only there would he would find true comfort, solace, and strength. Job's relationship with God was so strong that He could complain to Him, and in so doing, Job had an open heart that allowed him to enter into a conversation with God. While Cain became stuck in complaining, Job was able to move from complaining into a relationship.

> *"I had only heard about you before, but now I have seen you with my own eyes. I take back everything I said, and I sit in dust and ashes to show my repentance."* [12]

> Cain stayed in the graveyard, whereas Job entered into the garden. "So the Lord blessed Job in the second half of his life even more than in the beginning."[13]

As we journeyed through 2014, we had to choose how we were going to walk it out. I did dub it: "The Year from Hell," but Mark and I determined not to allow Satan a foothold as we processed. We made a deliberate decision not to ask God the *why* questions. The *why* question with God can get us caught in a trap.

We like to believe that we see the whole picture, but we don't. Therefore, we must make a conscious choice to relinquish that question and trust the One who does see the beginning, the end, and everything in-between. We forced ourselves to worship through the heartbreak and the tears. We asked Him to redeem the ground and propel our family forward. We intentionally entered into conversation with Him, asked Him how to pray, and how to move forward. We intentionally fought for our future and refused the potential bondage of complaining. It was not easy, but it was where our hope and future lay. We were determined to take the ground.

It is always our desire that our lives be pleasing to our Creator. Complaining and the *why* question would only hold us back. However, trust and worship would not only move us forward but would impact our family and those within our influence.

You may be wondering, what happened with our daughter. Donna wandered for a few years doing odd jobs that never quite fit. She attempted to get back into the professional horse arena, and even moved to another state to pursue that dream, only to have it come crashing down through a series of events that were once again beyond her control. Through the frustration and questions, God began to shift her toward a different path and further heal her heart. Today she is pursuing a career in nursing. God, in His faithfulness, took the areas of trauma and gently began to plant a garden. And, in Donna's case, I imagine that garden will someday include a horse to ride and to dream on. But someday is in the future.

> Conversations with God will always lead to godly wisdom in our lives.[14]

When my husband calls me on the phone, I don't have to ask who is calling because I know his voice even without caller ID. I know his voice because we have lived life together for over three decades.

God desires communication with us just as He did with Adam and Eve. God didn't go walking in the garden in the cool of the evening just because He felt like a stroll or needed exercise. He went walking in the garden in the cool of the evening because He desired to spend time with Adam and Eve. Because of the Fall, we all struggle to relate to God and to hear His voice. However, it doesn't have to be that way. When Jesus Christ died on the Cross, the veil in the temple was torn in half.[15] This signifies access to the heavenly realms which means that we have direct access to God. No longer do we need a priest to mediate for us because Jesus is our High Priest.[16] That division which formed when Adam and Eve sinned was conquered. I can hear God. You can hear God.

Throughout this chapter, we have talked a lot about positioning ourselves to trust God in the midst of each and every situation. One day, as I was praying, I saw mountains with valleys in the middle.

God reminded me that the only way to get to the next mountain is to go through the valley. He promises that He will take us from glory to glory, but what happens between the places of glory can be difficult. I love the scripture below because it reminds us that with God, we will survive.

When trauma hits, when life gets difficult, and when it feels like the world is caving in, God always gives me the precious gift of a passage of Scripture to hang onto. As you lean on the Word of God, it becomes the foundation that holds you up when you feel like your world is spinning out of control. If you are walking through trauma and looking for your garden, prayerfully read the following Scripture. In fact, own it; meditate on it and allow healing to pour over you. Our God is present, and He is faithful.

"All praise to God, the Father of our Lord Jesus Christ. God is our merciful Father and the source of all comfort. He comforts us in all our troubles so that we can comfort others. When they are troubled, we will be able to give them the same comfort God has given us. For the more we suffer for Christ, the more God will shower us with His comfort through Christ. Even when we are weighed down with troubles, it is for your comfort and salvation! For when we ourselves are comforted, we will certainly comfort you. Then you can patiently endure the same things we suffer. We are confident that as you share in our sufferings, you will also share in the comfort God gives us.

"We think you ought to know, dear brothers and sisters, about the trouble we went through in the province of Asia. We were crushed and overwhelmed beyond our ability to endure, and we thought we would never live through it. In fact, we expected to die. But as a result, we stopped relying on ourselves and learned to rely only

on God, who raises the dead. And He did rescue us from mortal danger, and He will rescue us again. We have placed our confidence in Him, and He will continue to rescue us. And you are helping us by praying for us. Then many people will give thanks because God has graciously answered so many prayers for our safety." [17]

God will always take us further than we believe we can go and give us greater impact than we believe we can have.

SPIRITUAL MUSCLE BUILDING

QUESTIONS

1. Trauma is different for everyone. What have you experienced in your life that feels like your own personal graveyard?

2. As you reflect on the first question, what keeps you in that place rather than walking in freedom?

ACTION STEPS

1. Put on some quiet worship music and ask Holy Spirit to minister deep into the core of your being, to wash over each and every area where the pain resides.

2. In your notebook, ask the Lord to speak words of encouragement and life to you as He removes the trauma.

3. Worship has tremendous power to move us through trauma in a

healthy manner. It repositions our focus to the One who is our comforter and our healer.

PRAYER AND DECLARATION

Heavenly Father, I thank You that You know everything that I have walked through. Nothing is hidden from You. I have many questions; however, I make a choice to release those questions to You and to trust You with my life. I ask Your forgiveness for any way I processed the trauma that did not align with Your Word. Where there has been death, destruction, disappointment, and failure, I ask You to breathe Your breath of life into those areas. Hope deferred makes the heart sick—so I command my heart, in the name of Jesus, to come to life and to become healthy. Your Word also says that dreams and desires that are fulfilled are like a tree of life. So, I thank You for life.

Heavenly Father, I release to You the times when I have felt forgotten. I ask Your forgiveness for the seasons where I have not focused on or trusted in You because I was hurting too much. I ask Your forgiveness for areas where I have allowed dreams to die. I give You permission to help me to dream again.

I decree and declare that I am made for the garden, not the graveyard. Father, I declare that You will take my greatest pain and find a way to use it for Your glory. I declare that I am not a victim; I am a victor. I decree and declare that I have the Host of Heaven on my side and I can live confidently that You are faithful and nothing can separate me from You.

SCRIPTURAL BASIS:

Proverbs 13:12, Romans 8:28-39

CHAPTER SEVEN
ROARING LIONS

"The Bible says that the devil is like a roaring lion (1 Peter 5:8). He comes in the darkness and tries to frighten the children of God with his mighty roar. But when you switch on the light of the Word of God, you discover that there is no lion. There is only a mouse with a microphone! The devil is an imposter. Got it?"[1]

REINHARD BONNKE

STRIKING A BALANCE

As we look at the whole issue of the demonic, there seems to be either an absolute denial of it or we blame everything on the demonic. However, like most situations, there is a balance. We must always pray for discernment. We ask God to reveal what has a demonic component behind it and what, in our belief system or culture, is coming against us. We never want to give too much attention to the demonic as that ultimately allows the enemy more power than what he really has. On the other hand, we do not want to dismiss the demonic either.

Yes. Demons do exist, and yes, they meddle in our lives. However, we can declare with Scripture, *"I belong to God; I am His dear child. I have already won a victory, because the Spirit who lives in me is greater than the spirit who lives in the world!"* [2]

In a previous chapter we talked about Job, however, what we didn't talk about was Satan requesting to commence an attack against this man of God.

> *"One day the members of the heavenly court came to present themselves before the Lord, and the Accuser, Satan, came with them. 'Where have you come from?' the Lord asked Satan. Satan answered the Lord, 'I have been patrolling the earth, watching everything that's going on.' Then the Lord asked Satan, 'Have you noticed my servant Job? He is the finest man in all the earth. He is blameless—a man of complete integrity. He fears God and stays away from evil.' Satan replied to the Lord, 'Yes, but Job has good reason to fear God. You have always put a wall of protection around him and his home and his property. You have made him prosper in everything he does. Look how rich he is! But reach out and take away everything he has, and he will surely curse you to your face!' 'All right, you may test him,' the Lord said to Satan. 'Do whatever you want with everything he possesses, but don't harm him physically.' So, Satan left the Lord's presence."* [3]

I don't understand why Almighty God allowed Job to be tested and I am one hundred percent sure that Job didn't appreciate it at all. However, I will say this, God trusted Job to remain focused and faithful.

Is my walk so exceptional that God will brag about me to my accuser?

Job was not warned that his test was coming, but Peter certainly was.

> *"Peter, my dear friend, listen to what I'm about to tell you. Satan has demanded to come and sift you like wheat and test your faith. But I have prayed for you, Peter, that you would stay faithful to me no matter what comes. Remember this: after you have turned back to me and have been restored, make it your life mission to strengthen the faith of your brothers."* [4]

Hindsight is an interesting thing. I am sure when Simon Peter reflected on that conversation, he realized that Jesus blatantly told him that he was going to fail the test. However, Jesus also assured him that He (Jesus) had prayed for him and that ultimately his (Peter's) faith would not fail. He also tells Peter that repentance will be necessary, but he will not be disqualified. Jesus also gave him an assignment to strengthen his brothers. During any test or attack, we need to be looking for our assignment in the situation.

> *"Stay alert! Watch out for your great enemy, the devil. He prowls around like a roaring lion, looking for someone to devour."* [5]

I love the word picture that Scripture paints. If you have ever watched a lion that is hunting, they are very focused and intent on finding their prey. A lion is looking for any vulnerability that will make the prey an easy target that can successfully be taken down. Likewise, the demonic agenda is to destroy us.

When God asked Satan what he had been up to, Satan responded, *"I have been patrolling the earth, watching everything that's going on."* [6] In other words, Satan was looking to cause trouble—trouble that would be intentional and very well executed. However, we have a battle plan. *"Stand firm against him (Satan), and be strong in your faith."*[7]

How do we stand firm when all hell is breaking loose and we feel like we are under attack? Great question! It is vital that we don't deny the attack; neither should we focus on the attack. Rather, we need to focus on God and the fact that we are in a spiritual battle knowing God will not allow us to enter a battle which we are not positioned to win. We must be very wise to not get sidetracked or distracted by the battle. In other words, we stand—we don't cave in—we don't hit the floor in despair and loss. We just stand. And, it's okay to call on some other believers to walk with us.

FINE-TUNED FOCUS

When we come under attack or experience transition in our lives, it is very easy to lose focus. We have all experienced falling back into our old habits and belief systems. And when we do, we swing open the door and allow fear and insecurity to come marching in, forgetting why we kicked them out in the first place. But, I want you to remember that God is always positioning us to see the way that He sees and to be aligned and empowered to walk into our divine destiny. We must choose to trust Him. In that decision, we make a choice to walk according to His path.

In Genesis, we have the account of Abraham's nephew, Lot, and his wife. Lot and his family separated from Abraham due to the combined number of animals that they had. Each needed more land to feed their livestock. Given first choice, Lot chose to settle his family in a very ungodly community.

In a previous chapter, we talked about an authentic relationship which includes communication. God actually took time to talk with Abraham about Sodom and Gomorrah,[8] the city where Lot settled. Abraham and God formed a close relationship. God told Abraham His plans and Abraham responded to God with confidence. When God wants to destroy the evil city, Abraham actually asks God, *"Will you sweep away both the righteous and the wicked?"*[9] He asks God to spare the city for fifty righteous, eventually talking Him down to just ten. This conversation could only happen because they intentionally cultivated a relationship. I suspect that Abraham believed that there certainly would be at least ten righteous people in that city since he stopped with ten. We must be secure enough in our relationship with God to continue communicating with Him, even in the midst of trials.

To summarize the story, because of His conversation with Abraham, God sends angels to the city to warn Lot. In this account, we see the wickedness of the city. However, I think what shines brightly is the love God has for His people. He had listened to Abraham and was willing to save the city for just ten righteous people. When ten people were not to be found, God sends His angels to rescue Lot. How great is the Father's love!

The angels tell Lot to gather his family and get out of town. Have you ever been in a situation where your family or extended family didn't believe you? That is exactly where Lot found himself. He told everyone to leave, and his extended family thinks he's lost his mind! Sadly, Lot hesitates rather than heeding the urgent warning of the angels. In the end, the angels grab him and he flees the town with only his wife and daughters.

> God will always have a plan for our escape; the
> challenge is to follow it the entire way through.

"When they were safely out of the city, one of the angels ordered, 'Run for your lives! And don't look back or stop anywhere in the valley! Escape to the mountains, or you will be swept away!' 'On no, my lord!' Lot begged. 'You have been so gracious to me and saved my life, and you have shown such great kindness. But I cannot go to the mountains. Disaster would catch up with me there, and I would soon die. See, there is a small village nearby. Please let me go there instead; don't you see how small it is? Then my life will be saved.'" [10]

I suspect that Lot was comfortable with the nearby village. However, God was calling him higher into the mountains. Lot did not have the confidence in God to obey Him. God's plan and strategy in our lives is always best. We may not understand, but God sees the bigger picture.

The story later tells us that Lot's daughters realize that there are no men left to give them children, which was a huge disgrace for women of that time. So, they get their father drunk and have sex with him.

I have to wonder what the outcome would have been if Lot had gone to the mountain and followed God's plan. The village was Lot's plan. How often do we stop short of the fullness of God because we invite fear and insecurity to join us in unsettling moments? How many doors do we unknowingly open for demonic schemes when we don't go the distance with God? All of Lot's reasoning made sense to him in his comfort zone and earthly realm. Despite being rescued by

God, Lot was unable to see from a spiritual perspective. He chose not to trust God with the fullness of God's plan.

However, the pain doesn't stop there. When God tells us to run or to move, we need to take heed not to look back. Step forward with trusting obedience.

> *"Lot reached the village just as the sun was rising over the horizon. Then the Lord rained down fire and burning sulfur from the sky on Sodom and Gomorrah. He utterly destroyed them, along with the other cities and villages of the plain, wiping out all the people and every bit of vegetation. But Lot's wife looked back as she was following behind him, and she turned into a pillar of salt."* [11]

A subtle, but effective demonic trap is to tempt us to look back and hang onto the past rather than hanging onto God and running towards our future. It can be so easy to allow fear and insecurity to sneak back in, like a thief climbing in through an open window. Or we may try to put on our superhero cape, complete with the mask and run headlong into our kryptonite, forgetting that God has a bigger plan and that He will get us through everything that is coming against us. We dwell on the ungodly belief systems and labels that we carry from the past. And, sometimes as we look back, we deceive ourselves into thinking that the past was better (more comfortable) than our future.

As I have journeyed through life, I have learned over and over how subtle and highly effective this trap can be. As Lot and his wife ran, she didn't keep her focus on the safe place where God was taking them. Instead she looked back and tried to hang onto the past.

In my case, I may move forward, but then I may look back as soon as I am uncomfortable with where God is taking me. What happens is interesting. When I look back, I tend to change the situation and romanticize how things could have been if I had stayed there. This is essentially what Lot's wife did.

Even with angels pulling her by the hand, she still wanted to hang onto the past. We must remember where God is taking us will always be a bit uncomfortable because it is unfamiliar, but that doesn't mean that He has not equipped us to walk into new territory. We can also be assured that as we enter that new territory, He will expose any beliefs that do not align with Him and where He is taking us. He will also be right there, asking with a smile, "Do you see what I see?"

In 2017, I resigned a full-time pastoral position within my local church. My spirit had been unsettled for some time and I knew that the season was shifting and at some point I would resign. I had a lot of relationships there and had been part of that body for a very long time. As God said, *"Now"*, there was also a warning. He knows me well and knew how much I enjoyed many aspects of pastoring in that community. He knew that I would grieve deeply even as I moved forward with anticipation and excitement into what He was calling me to.

The Holy Spirit impressed me very strongly that there would be a temptation to look back, but that it was a trap. If I was going to move forward into a new season full of new adventure, I could not allow myself to look back and hang onto the past. If I did that, I would forfeit my destiny just as Lot's wife had done. In addition, I could not beg to go only part way, like Lot did. I needed to go the distance. Whenever we are taking new territory, there will always be a demonic scheme designed to hold us back and make us ineffective. There will always be some level of unease when we are taking new ground, however, that doesn't necessarily mean the ground is not to be taken.

THE EVER AFTER

It amazes me that when we talk about demonic assaults, we talk about Job, all his pain and all that he lost. There is so much pain throughout his story that we often forget to look at what happened on the other side. God allowed Job to walk through the demonic attack and schemes that were meant to take him down. God had confidence that Job would make it to the other side, and Job did.

> *"So the Lord blessed Job in the second half of his life even more than in the beginning. For now, he had 14,000 sheep, 6,000 camels, 1,000 teams of oxen, and 1,000 female donkeys. He also gave Job seven more sons and three more daughters. He named his first daughter Jeminah, the second Keziah, and the third Keren-happuch. In all the land no women were as lovely as the daughters of Job. And their father put them into his will along with their brothers. Job lived 140 years after that, living to see four generations of his children and grandchildren. Then he died, an old man who had lived a long, full life."* [12]

Names are very important in the Bible. There are some clues to be found as we look at Job's name and the names of the daughters that were born after Satan's attack.

Job's name means: "the persecuted; hated; one ever returning to God; he that weeps; a desert; (root= to persecute; to be an enemy)." [13]

What jumps out at me in that definition is *one ever returning to God.* That is a powerful statement. Is our walk with God such that we are ever returning to God, in every season of our lives? Scripture doesn't tell us Job's wife's name, nor the names of the children he lost in the first half of his life. However, we do have the names of his daughters that were born later. Their names reveal where Job's heart was.

1. Jemina (je-mi'-mah) – Dove; a little dove. Daily. He will spoil (mar) her.[14]

2. Kezia (ke-zi'-ah) = Cassia; i.e. equally as precious; (root+ to scrape to peel off).[15]

3. Keren-happuch [Keren-Happuch] (ke'-ren-hap'-puk) = Beautifier or horn of paint; a horn reserved; the horn or child of beauty.[16]

To summarize, I see Job, a man who was persecuted but always returned to God and ultimately persecuted the Enemy. As God restores Job's life, there is nothing in his daughters' names that reflect anything other than love and praise to God. Jeminah, the *little dove*. Remember, in the New Testament the dove represents Holy Spirit. We have Keziah who is *equally as precious*. The second part of the definition for her name talks about scraping off. Sometimes we have to scrape off the junk that we have accumulated from a bout with the demonic. We were not created to carry it, and if we try to, it holds us back and makes us less effective or takes us out altogether.

As Job walked forward with his life, I believe he was in awe of the goodness and beauty of God. He refused to carry anything from the past that would hold him back from his future. When we seek God first, He will reveal anything that we have been slimed with. The third daughter, Keren-happuch uses the term *horn*. Often in Scripture a horn represents strength and honor. Job walked through the remainder of his life with strength and honor that could only come from a deep trust in God.

God called Job *"the finest man of earth."* What does God say of me?

Ultimately, Scripture tells us that Job was more blessed in the second half of his life. Remember Peter? He failed as he denied Jesus three times, yet Jesus restored him and the shock waves from that victory still reverberate today. This man, who was quick to open his mouth and deny Jesus, also developed a boldness that spread the Word of God far and wide.

We all know that the attacks can seem relentless. This passage in Ephesians has become a foundational basis for me whenever I encounter demonic schemes.

"In conclusion, be strong in the Lord [draw your strength from Him and be empowered through your union with Him] and in the power of His [boundless] might. Put on the full armor of God [for His precepts are like the splendid armor of a heavily-armed soldier], so that you may be able to [successfully] stand up against all the schemes and the strategies and the deceits of the devil. For our struggle is not against flesh and blood [contending only with physical opponents], but against the rulers, against the powers, against the world forces of this [present] darkness, against the spiritual forces of wickedness in the heavenly (supernatural) places. Therefore, put on the complete armor of God, so that you will be able to [successfully] resist and stand your ground in the evil day [of danger], and having done everything [that the crisis demands], to stand firm [in your place, fully prepared, immovable, victorious]." [17]

> Walking through demonic schemes, without letting go of God, always leads to victory!

When we are combating demonic schemes, the very least we are expected to do is stand firm. However, even greater than that, we have the ability to take ground in the midst of an attack. To do this, we may have to take a radically focused stance and refuse to give up any ground.

COLLISION

I had just completed a women's conference in another state. It had been a time of intense teaching and ministry. I still remember one young lady standing in front of me with tears running down her face as the spirits of death, dying, and suicide were broken off and she experienced the love of God for the first time.

I was on the final stretch driving home. Somewhere I once read that most accidents happen within twenty-five miles from home. I was about to experience that and become another statistic. It was a dark, rainy night and difficult to see the road ahead. The next thing I knew, I did a face plant in the airbag. But I was alive and so was the driver in the other car.

Then, it began to get strange. As the other driver stepped out of his car, I noticed his shirt. It was a dark colored shirt with a demonic face on it. I choose to pay little heed to the demonic. I fully understand that all power and authority belong to Jesus; however, there was something in the atmosphere. That shirt was making a statement and I was working hard to ignore it. Some people just wear clothing with demonic symbols on them. At that moment, all I realized was something was off; however, I now know that it was a Holy Spirit warning. There was more behind the shirt than could be seen in the natural.

It wasn't long before one of his buddies arrived. He literally came bounding on the scene, full of excitement, and yelling, "Your neck hurts right? Your back hurts, right?" It seemed like there was no end to his enthusiasm.

At that point, I called a friend who lived nearby. She and her husband immediately came to the scene of the accident. There are some battles, some attacks, where we need others to stand with us no matter how strong we think we are. Although my husband was on his way, I quickly realized that I needed someone to stand with me as I waited. What was unfolding at that accident scene was bizarre and I needed to call in another believer to stand with me until Mark arrived.

LEGAL MATTERS

It wasn't that long after the car accident that the insurance company notified me that I was being sued. In some ways, this rocked me more than the actual accident had. My husband's business had been falsely sued a few years prior to that. I knew what it took to walk through that, and here we were again. If you've been in a legal battle, you know that it can feel like you have little to no control. This is the same feeling that we often have when we are up against a demonic battle or demonic scheme. As I processed the lawsuit, I found my mind going through all the maybes that went along with it. God gave us wonderful imaginations when used correctly. However, they can also become a place for a downward spiral.

As I found my footing, I went before the Lord and asked Him for peace. Spending time with the Lord to process what is happening in life provides the keys and strategies that change everything. The Holy Spirit led me to Luke 6:28 NLT. "*Bless those who curse you. Pray for those who hurt you.*" It immediately became clear that I needed to follow the Scripture that says, "*We destroy every proud obstacle that keeps people from knowing God. We capture their rebellious thoughts and teach them to obey Christ.*"[18]

My job was to wrestle and hold down any thoughts that did not align with God. In other words, all the thoughts that provoked ill feelings toward the other party, fear, insecurity, or panic, all had to be taken captive. These thoughts needed to be brought into alignment with the Word of God. I learned that I needed to focus on Scriptures like Psalm 91 which speak directly to the issue of fear, God's provision and protection. As I began to do this, God gave me another key. He asked me to intentionally speak and pray blessing over the individual who was bringing the lawsuit. So, as I *caught each thought,* I turned around and spoke a blessing instead. At first this felt very forced and rote but eventually, that prayer of blessing became easy and my attitude came into submission with the very heartbeat of God.

I was attending a conference in California and was sound asleep when the phone rang at 4:00 am. As I looked at the caller-ID, I realized it was my attorney calling. I hesitantly answered the phone. She informed me that the other individual had called them and asked to settle out of court. She said that the individual apologized for everything, including wanting to go through the lawsuit. She said, "It's over." I just laid there, pondering the outcome. Everything up to that point had been full of vengeance. God tells us to bless and not to curse.

> When we position ourselves to bless rather than curse,
> or be held captive by fear, the meddling schemes of
> the enemy lose their power and authority.

When we are engaged in battle, our focus must be rightly glued to heavenly, not earthly, realms. Remember the previous chapter about our sticky value? As we grow in God, we become rightly glued, and our sticky value to the things of Christ increases. Our focus becomes fixed. The best image I can think of is a horse with blinders on. Those blinders narrow the field of vision. Our field of vision needs to be focused on and in the heavenly realms because that is where we receive strength and provision for the journey. And it is from that focus that God will give us needed strategies to win the battle we are facing. The author of Hebrews gives us a great leveling field.

"So consider carefully how Jesus faced such intense opposition from sinners who opposed their own souls, so that you won't become worn down and cave in under life's pressures." [19]

POWER PLAY

We must become adept at intentionally focusing on God. Equally, we the need an accurate scriptural understanding. Satan loves to take Scripture out of context and use it against us. If he did it with Jesus, how much more will he try that with us?

"Then Jesus was led by the Spirit into the wilderness to be tempted there by the devil. For forty days and forty nights He fasted and became very hungry. During that time the devil came and said to Him, 'If you are the Son of God, tell these stones to become loaves of bread.' But Jesus told him, 'No! The Scriptures say, 'People do not live by bread alone, but by every word that comes from the mouth of God.'

"Then the devil took Him to the old city, Jerusalem, to the highest point of the Temple, and said, 'If you are the Son of God, jump

off! For the Scriptures say, 'He will order His angels to protect You. And they will hold You up with their hands, so You won't even hurt Your foot on a stone." Jesus responded, 'The Scriptures also say, 'You must not test the Lord your God."

"Next the devil took Him to the peak of a very high mountain and showed Him all the kingdoms of the world and their glory. 'I will give it all to You,' he said, 'if You will kneel down and worship me.' 'Get out of here, Satan,' Jesus told him. 'For the Scriptures say, 'You must worship the Lord your God and serve only him.' Then the devil went way, and angels came and took care of Jesus." [20]

Remember how Satan asked permission to test Job? Do you recall when Jesus told Peter that he would be sifted like wheat? We tend to miss the truth that Jesus was *led by the Spirit* into the wilderness. Just stop there for a moment.

The Holy Spirt was responsible for putting Jesus in a position where He would be tempted by Satan himself. Most of the time when we are dealing with demons, the Son of God will deal directly with Satan. When we really ponder this, it gives a whole new understanding to the following Scripture passage.

"This is why he had to be a Man and take hold of our humanity in every way. He made us his brothers and sisters and became our merciful and faithful King-Priest before God; as the One who removed our sins to make us one with him." [18] "He suffered and endured every test and temptation, so that he can help us every time we pass through the ordeals of life." [21]

When my kids were little, I would say that I could do anything if I had enough sleep. Jesus was hungry and tired, yet His focus remained on His Father. He knew His assignment; He understood Scripture; and He could not be moved. We need to be focused like He was.

This Scripture helps put things into perspective as we read,

> *"We all experience times of testing, which is normal for every human being. But God will be faithful to you. He will screen and filter the severity, nature, and timing of every test or trial you face so that you can bear it. And each test is an opportunity to trust him more, for along with every trial God has provided for you a way of escape that will bring you out of it victoriously."* [22]

Isolation is one of Satan's strategies to get us to believe that we are alone and that no one understands. However, when we keep our focus, we recognize that this is a lie. Jesus was able to keep His focus, and ultimately, Satan had no choice but to leave Him. Why? Because Jesus could not be budged. As we draw closer to God, we see with His eyes. When we see with His eyes, demonic schemes are revealed. Satan loves to get our focus off the Lord and sees that as victory. Sometimes, we may have to fight to keep our focus, but, the battle is well worth it. Always remember, God wins!

What subtle lie does Satan use to try and distract my focus?

Am I standing so firm that Satan has no choice but to leave?

Someone once said that Jesus was led into the wilderness by the Holy Spirit but came out with power. When we are walking with God, we do not need to fear the demonic. We should expect that a child of God who properly handles a demonic scheme will come out the other side with power and victory.

Child of the Living God, you have the full force of the heavenly realms in your corner. The war has already been won. These are only side-line skirmishes. Know that the full force of the Kingdom of Heaven is with you; therefore, the odds are totally in your favor. Keep your focus, for the True Force of the armies of heaven is with you.

SPIRITUAL MUSCLE BUILDING

QUESTIONS

1. What has my attitude been when thinking about and/or dealing with the demonic?

2. Do I believe that Satan has as much power and authority as God does? Why or why not?

ACTION STEPS

1. We often ascribe the same attributes to Satan as those belonging to God.

   a. I would encourage you to search out Scripture and see what it says about Satan, demons and their power and authority.

   b. Then take time to search Scripture about God. Focus primarily on what was accomplished when Jesus died on the Cross.

2. What difference does a proper understanding of God's power and authority versus Satan's power and authority make in my life?

3. Take time to worship and give thanks to God. Worship is a powerful weapon of warfare. So, next time you feel like you are in a battle, how about some worship!

PRAYER AND DECLARATION

Heavenly Father, I ask Your forgiveness for the times when I have acted as if the demonic is more powerful than You are. I ask for Your forgiveness when I have allowed the demonic to hinder what You have called me to do. By the power and authority of the True Lord Jesus Christ, I take back all rights and authority that I have given to the demonic realm. I proclaim that I belong to Jesus and that no weapon formed against me shall prosper. I align myself with the full Kingdom of Heaven and I declare that Satan was defeated at the Cross. I declare that I will not be unaware of the schemes of Satan but will be empowered by the Word of God. I will not live in fear of the demonic because I walk with Jesus and that war has already been won. Therefore, I declare that I am strong in the Lord and in His power! Because of Jesus, I can take my stand against the demonic schemes and no weapon formed against me will prosper!

SCRIPTURAL BASIS:

1 John 4:4, 2 Corinthians 2:11, Ephesians 6:8-10, Isaiah 54:7

MOMENTS AND MOUNTAIN MOVING

"The power of God will take you out of your own plans
and put you into the plan of God."[1]
SMITH WIGGLESWORTH

A MOMENT CHANGES EVERYTHING

"Trust in the Lord completely, and do not rely on your own opinions. With all your heart rely on him to guide you, and he will lead you in every decision you make. Become intimate with him in whatever you do, and he will lead you wherever you go. Don't think for a moment that you know it all." [2]

Walking with God is always a journey. In my experience, that journey is never a straight line. God loves to show us many things along our way. He is the master tour guide who knows every stop, every treasure, every unique sight along the path. He guides with the enthusiasm of a Father who has an awesome, treasured, and valuable surprise gift for His child. He is so focused on the journey with us that if we miss something the first time, He will take us around again until we see it as He sees it.

As He talks with us, He also invites us to dream with Him. We talk and dream—dream and talk—and we learn. Being the wonderful planner, God also has things all worked out for us to walk into a new season at just the opportune moment. We simply have to trust Him and walk with Him.

I love the different streams that flow within the Body of Christ. I think we all have our stream that we are most comfortable in. The church where I was on staff usually invited guest teachers and preachers from a specific stream to speak. Purposefully, I tend to go fishing in other streams when I look for speakers. I am desperate for the *whole* that the body of Christ has to offer. Let me be clear. Anyone I take into consideration to teach has to be aligned with the Word of God; I do not budge on that one. I well remember Patricia King making a statement that there are certain fundamental doctrines that we have to agree on (i.e. Jesus is the Son of God, etc.). However, there are other areas that are a bit gray. Within the body, we need to have some give and take while still diligently aligning with the Word of God.

> *"For we have the living Word of God, which is full of energy, and it pierces more sharply than a two-edged sword. It will even penetrate to the very core of our being where soul and spirit, bone and marrow meet! It interprets and reveals the true thoughts and secret motives of our hearts."* [3]

When I think of *alive and powerful*, I think of movement, adventure, and learning. The only way we can truly journey with God is face forward, which will ultimately propel us forward.

In 2016, I invited Patricia King to speak at our woman's conference. Little did I realize that God was going to use this conference, and this woman of God, to catapult me into a *kairos* moment. A *kairos* moment is defined as, "*a time when conditions are right for the accomplishment of a crucial action: the opportune and decisive moment.*"[4]

For years, I had a repeated prophetic word over my life. I'd heard the initial word and received a call into ministry while I was at the Toronto Airport Christian Fellowship many years before. As the years went on, I would hear the word again through both well-known prophetic voices and not so well-known prophetic voices. I began to joke that God just had to hit the play button to give me a prophetic word. Little did I know that when Patricia King came on the scene, God hit the play button and the season shifted. In this case, what was once a *future* word suddenly became a *now* word.

Looking back, I realize that I was not aimlessly roaming for all those years. God had me on a planned journey. We were stopping, studying, learning and healing along the way. Yes, I even got battered and bruised in the process. However, God was faithful to use that for my good as well. As we journeyed together, God was healing my heart and teaching me to keep a short account of wrongs. He was teaching me to be a leader and increasing my wisdom. He was teaching me to pack differently, that I didn't need all the painful baggage that I was trying to carry. I needed only the tools that He would equip me with. He was teaching me to use new skill sets and providing mentors along the way. He was teaching me to dream with Him, to utter His prophecies, adjusting my identity to align with His, and pulling me out of my comfort zone over and over.

It can be easy to feel like we have been abandoned and left on the bench where God can't use us. In reality, He is preparing us in ways we could not even imagine. With that said, know this. You have not been forgotten or overlooked. Hang onto Him, grow in His Word, develop your relationship with Him, and walk into your destiny.

At one point, I remember the Lord speaking to me during my quiet time. He told me to allow myself to dream with Him and to see where He was taking me in the spiritual realm. I needed to be able to grab hold of it in the spirit before it would manifest on earth. I didn't have man's credentials to get to the place where He was calling me. I had been reminded over and over that I didn't have the right credentials for what I was doing. This insecurity was well ingrained within me and a battle that had to be fought. However, when God says go, it is best to go, and trust Him to give you wisdom and favor in the journey. I couldn't make things happen, but God...

RADICAL FAITH IN ACTION

There are many people throughout Scripture who were able to look past the immediate moment. One of my favorites is Rahab. This amazing woman was a Gentile living an ungodly lifestyle. However, she seemed to know there must be something more, and she was willing to exercise radical faith in a God she didn't know, to reach past the present and into the future. When she made the decision to lower the spies down through her window, everything in her life changed. Not only was she rescued as her city was destroyed, but she was also adopted into the Israelite community and is one of the women listed in the genealogy of Jesus Christ.

This amazes me for several reasons. She was female, and women were not traditionally counted in any way, much less listed in a genealogy. Rahab was a Gentile, not from Jewish descent, which is another reason she shouldn't be listed in Jesus' genealogy from a human standpoint. This tells me that God is more interested in our future than we realize. The decisions that we make in a moment often have the potential to impact future generations in ways we never envisioned. Rahab's decision changed the trajectory of her life and the lives of her descendants.

Mary, the mother of Jesus, is another radical woman of God. This young Jewish girl would become fuel for gossip in her community and beyond. How many times have we made assumptions or operated on perceptions about people without knowing the full story? I wonder how many people stopped to ask Mary how she became pregnant. How many of us would ask that question? I'm pretty sure we know how a woman gets pregnant. Mary was willing to risk everything to move forward with God. Would you respond to the angel of the Lord the way Mary did?

> *"Then Mary responded, saying, 'This is amazing! I will be a mother for the Lord! As his servant, I accept whatever he has for me. May everything you have told me come to pass.' And the angel left her."* 5

A moment with God most certainly changes everything. Often, God's effects cause a radical change. For instance, Mary's obedience changed the world.

We've looked at some women, but we cannot forget about the men who radically followed God. We have our much-loved account of Daniel, a young man living in a foreign land. Because he refused to bow down and worship the king, he was thrown into the lions' den. Daniel was so focused on God that the lions, who were supposed to attack him, became kitty cats. Basically, the roar of the earthly lion becomes the purr of a kitten when the Host of Heaven comes on the scene. This account reminded us of the protection and provision of God. But how many of us would be so focused on God, so secure in our identity, and so determined to trust God that we refused to bow down? Let's go one step further…

> How many of us could hang out with
> ravenous lions in a state of peace?

FINAL SAY

We must realize that even when life doesn't make sense, God can make beauty and work everything for His glory and for our good. If you have ever made anything, you know that a work in process looks nothing like the end result.

Isaiah 54 is a prophetic word that looks ahead to the restoration and salvation of Israel, but it also outlines how we feel when our heart is heavy. "*O storm-battered city, troubled and desolate!*"[6] The key during seasons of pain is not to see trouble and desolation. At this point, we must not fall back and retreat rather than move forward. In Exodus, as the people knew the Egyptian army was coming up behind them, the Red Sea was in front of them, Moses reminded them, "*Don't be afraid. Just stand still and watch the Lord rescue you today… The Lord Himself will fight for you. Just stay calm.*"[7] We need to fight fear, continue to stand, trust the Lord to fight, and stay in a place of peace.

A key component to facing and moving forward is to allow peace to invade, inhabit and control our very atmosphere. Think again about the Israelites knowing that the Egyptian army was fast approaching. "*You will not leave in a hurry, running for your lives. For the Lord will go ahead of you; yes, the God of Israel will protect you from behind."*[8] The picture of protection from behind is that of a rear guard, which is a military term. We don't have to look behind us, because God has our backs and will fight for us. I would also suggest that being told not to leave in a hurry is not procrastination, but the idea of getting ready to go and making the journey peacefully with the focus on God who guides the way. Focus has a major impact on how we view the journey through life on this earth.

In areas of wounding, it is vital to allow God's healing reach deeply into the core of our being. We were not meant to carry the baggage of our past into a God-ordained future. Yes, we can romanticize the past when the future looks impossible. We may say that hindsight is 20/20, but it can also be a trap that pulls us backward rather than propelling us forward. When we are tied to the past, it should be a warning that we are not moving forward.

As a leader, there have been many times when I am quaking inside. During these times, it is not unusual for the words coming out of my mouth to be very different than my words going up to God! This was the case with Moses as he faced the Red Sea.

> *"Then the Lord said to Moses, 'Why are you crying out to Me? Tell the people to get moving! Pick up your staff and raise your hand over the sea. Divide the water so the Israelites can walk through the middle of the sea on dry ground.'"*[9]

Moses had to make a decision. He could be overwhelmed by the army coming from behind; he could be swayed by popular opinion and fear; or he could listen to God and use the tools he was given. What were the tools that Moses had in his arsenal? The tools he was given included a history of God's faithfulness, and a stick. Moses had to trust in the faithfulness of God, look at the sea, and take authority over it using a stick.

Often, at the point of our greatest pain, frustration, discouragement, or failure is when we attempt to live in the past rather than positioning ourselves to move forward into the future. We must learn to take the tools that we have and trust God to use them in ways we never imagined, even if that tool is only a stick.

BECOMING MIGHTY

If we want to become mighty, we must learn to move mountains. Understand that a mountain is anything that stands between us and God's intended purpose.

> "...I promise you, if you have faith inside of you no bigger than the size of a small mustard seed, you can say to this mountain, 'Move away from here and go over there,' and you will see it move! There is nothing you couldn't do!" [10]

Throughout this book we have talked about David. One of the many interesting things about David is that many of the men who would team up with this future king were outcasts and discontented trouble-makers. He didn't run with those we would consider the cream of the crop. I suspect that if these men had walked into many of our churches, we would have been on very high alert and calling the police. However, these men developed mountain-moving skills. These men were known as David's Mighty Men. Of those, there were three who really stood out who we would refer to them as the mightiest of the mighty men.

> "These are the names of David's mightiest warriors. The first was Jashobeam the Hacmonite, who was the leader of the Three – the

*three mightiest warriors among David's men. He once used his
spear to kill 800 enemy warriors in a single battle."* [11]

Whether we are moving mountains or going to war, the victorious
believer is the one who has a heart committed to the mission and
the courage to carry it out. Jashobeam means, *"He will return among
the people; the people return to God."* [12] Hacmonite means, *"very wise;
(root=to be wise; to be cunning; to be skillful)."* [13] Jashobeam only had
a spear to use against the enemy warriors.

Our faith in God and our small measures of simple every day
obedience build up to a critical mass for breakthrough and mountain
moving. When we focus on God, He is faithful and we will have more
than enough to move the mountain. We can assume that Jashobeam
leaned into God, received His vast wisdom, and the day was won. Do
we have the single focus, determination, and commitment to keep
the course until we reach critical mass and experience breakthrough?

*"Next in rank among the Three was Eleazar son of Dodai, a
descendant of Ahoah. Once Eleazar and David stood together
against the Philistines when the entire Israelite army had fled.
He killed Philistines until his hand was too tired to lift his sword,
and the Lord gave him a great victory that day. The rest of the
army did not return until it was time to collect the plunder!"* [14]

Note that Eleazar fought with such intensity that the sword stuck to
his hand. In Scripture, the sword often represents the Word of God.
Jesus used the Word of God as a sword to defeat Satan when He
declared, *"It is written."* [15] Eleazar means, *"whom God helps or aids; the
help of God; God is helper."* [16] Dodo (or Dodai) is Hebrew for *"beloved
of the LORD; Jehovah is loving. His beloved."* [17] And finally, Ahohite
is a word meaning *"brother of rest."* [18] If we boil this down, we have a

man who is secure in his relationship to God (helper and beloved), walks in peace (rest), and is able to do warfare from a standpoint of love for his brothers (and sisters). Are we so determined and loyal that our hand becomes one with the Word of God?

> *"For although we live in the natural realm, we don't wage a military campaign employing human weapons, using manipulation to achieve our aims. Instead, our spiritual weapons are energized with divine power to effectively dismantle the defenses behind which people hide."* [19]

Are we able to do warfare from a position of love for our brothers and sisters?

David and Eleazar stood together. This is a key point. Standing indicates the refusal to give in no matter how difficult the situation may appear and how outnumbered we may be. *"Put on all of God's armor so that you will be able to stand firm against all strategies of the devil."* [20] The word *stand*, as used here, is active not passive. And I would suggest it is a permanent stance, not a temporary one. We are to look at each situation with confidence knowing that when we are united with God, we are on the winning team.

> *"Next in rank was Shammah son of Agee from Harar. One time the Philistines gathered at Lehi and attacked the Israelites in a field full of lentils. The Israelite army fled, but Shammah held his ground in the middle of the field and beat back the Philistines. So the Lord brought about a great victory."* [21]

Notice that Shammah is commended for defending a bean field. Why? Because he understood that this lentil patch was a strategic position in battle and would be a source of provision for generations to come.

There is one additional comment I want to make regarding Shammah. The name Shammah means *"astonishment; desolation; loss; root+to be astonished; to lay waste; to make desolate."* [22] Some of us believe that because of the hand dealt to us, we have no great impact. The other two men that we discussed in this section have powerful names. Shammah's name would represent desolation and loss. However, that name did not define Shammah. He was looking ahead into an intended future and defending the land.

What decisions am I making in this moment? Are they decisions that will bring death and destruction to future generations? OR am I defending the proverbial bean field to ensure provision for generations to come?

David's mighty men had conditioned their minds for victory. They did not allow their past to define their future. What is defining my future? What defines yours?

Paul so wonderfully sums this up as he writes,

> *"I don't depend on my own strength to accomplish this; however, I do have one compelling focus: I forget all of the past as I fasten my heart to the future instead. I run straight for the divine invitation of reaching the heavenly goal and gaining the victory-prize through the anointing of Jesus."* [23]

When we walk in relationship with the living God, we understand that we are headed for something better. We understand that God has given us what we need to walk into our future. However, we must actually move forward for it to happen. Someone once said that we *must decide* to focus on Jesus because every other focus leads to death and destruction.

Going back to Isaiah 54 *"...I will rebuild you with precious jewels and make your foundation from lapis lazuli."*[24] If something requires rebuilding, we can safely assume that it was damaged in the first place. As we have walked through life, the acid of our past has eroded our foundations. There may be foundation blocks missing. Or, we may have become comfortable in our past, sat down, and stopped looking ahead to the future. God always looks at the whole.

Rebuilding a foundation requires work. The old joint mortar has to be removed, dirt and grime washed away, and the cracked stones or blocks removed. No matter what the sticky value is of the ungodly beliefs that we carry, God is able to remove them. And, He is more than able to strengthen and increase the sticky value of the beliefs that align with His Word which we need to carry with us. God has the original blueprints and is very adept at reading them.

Isaiah refers to the foundations being built from lapis lazuli. This was a most sought-after stone, the symbol of royalty and honor, God's power and vision, and was considered a universal symbol of wisdom and truth.

God desires to rebuild *our* foundation. Our identity is that of royalty and honor. We are called to walk in wholeness and the power of God. We are to see from heaven's perspective, which is full of wisdom and truth. God is faithful to rebuild us using only the best materials. He is so good that we can be assured He will never do sub-standard work. He will always uphold His end of the deal as He has promised.

Children of the King, heirs to the Kingdom of Heaven, do not wear hand-me-downs. You are not second-class citizens, nor do you eat the crumbs under the banquet table. No! Children of the King are created to wear priestly garments, to be first class citizens, and to eat at the banqueting table. We are created to be mighty men and women of God!

SPIRITUAL MUSCLE BUILDING

QUESTIONS

1. What mountains in my life need moving?

2. Are there areas where I am allowing my past to define my future?

ACTION STEPS

1. Commit time to know God, your Father. Study the Scriptures. Talk to God as you would talk to a valued and special friend. Remember to take time to listen. Write down what you hear and make sure it aligns with Scripture.

2. Write down this verse and carry it with you. Meditate on it and follow what it says to your spirit. *Your own ears will hear Him. Right behind you a voice will say, "This is the way you should go," Whether to the right or to the left.* (Isaiah 30:21 NLT)

3. Commit to TRUST. Carry this verse with you also and allow it to go deep into your being. *Trust in the Lord with all your heart; do not depend on your own understanding. Seek His will in all you do, and He will show you which path to take.* (Proverbs 3:5-6 NLT)

Walking with God is always a journey. Through my experience, I know my journey is not a straight line. God loves to show me many things along the way. He is the Master tour guide who knows every stop, every treasure, and every unique site. He guides with an enthusiasm of a Father who has an awesome, treasured, valuable surprise gift for His child waiting around every corner.

> He is so focused on the journey with us that if we miss something the first time, He will take us around again until we see it as He sees it.

He has not given up, so don't you give up. He WILL show you which path to take.

PRAYER AND DECLARATION

Heavenly Father, when I look to You, I know You will make my path straight. I thank You that I don't have to trust my understanding and wisdom, but I can trust Yours. I thank You that You will never give up on me. In each and every situation, I trust I can look to You.

Therefore, I declare that I am a child of the Living God and a fellow heir with Christ. I am valued and worthy. I declare that no weapon formed against me will prosper because I belong to You. I commit to the study of Your Word and I declare that the Word of God will be welded to my hand as my sword. I commit to pour out the love (fragrance) of God to those around me that they may encounter the Living God through me.

SCRIPTURAL BASIS:
Proverbs 3:5-6, Isaiah 54:7, John 1:12,
Romans 8:17, 2 Corinthians 2:14

CONCLUSION

"We were not created to be average or mediocre. We have been summoned by God and empowered by His Spirit to step out of the crowd and be counted among the brave. We must refuse to hide among the riskless, mindless, zombielike flock. We must put on the mind of Christ and expose the world to the supernatural wisdom of the ages—wisdom that stuns the intelligent, silences the critics and transforms our cities and nations. Jesus said that we are to make disciples of all nations and teach them the ways of the Kingdom."[1]

KRIS VALLOTTON

Have you ever watched a show where a person is drowning in quicksand? They are walking along and suddenly, down they go. The more they struggle, the deeper they go until eventually, they disappear beneath the surface. Of course, because we like suspense, their hat is likely to remain perched on top of the quicksand. Unfortunately, television and movies have not given us an accurate description of how quicksand works.

"Quicksand—that is, sand that behaves as a liquid because it is saturated with water—can be a mucky nuisance, but it's basically impossible to die in the way that is depicted in movies. That's because quicksand is denser than the human body. People and animals can get stuck in it, but they don't get sucked down to the bottom – they float on the surface. Our legs are pretty dense, so they may sink, but the torso contains the lungs, and thus is buoyant enough to stay out of trouble."[2]

When we feel like we are stuck in old habits, wounding, and beliefs, we can feel like we are being swallowed by quicksand with no hope of rescue. This is what the demonic wants us to believe and sometimes what our minds do believe as truth. We become convinced that we are in a hopeless situation with no place to go but down. However, our God always has an escape plan; not only an escape plan, but a plan for us to flourish. He is an expert at rebuilding every area of our damaged lives which may be holding us back from being the person He created us to be. We can be assured that *Not one promise from God is empty of power, for nothing is impossible with God!*[3] and that the first part of that process is to lean back into Him.

As I researched, I Googled what to do if I got stuck in quicksand. Since my exposure was through the media, my impression was that if you're in quicksand, you're in a hopeless situation, but I was wrong. *"If you do find yourself stuck in quicksand, the best idea is to lean back so that the weight of your body is distributed over a wider area. Moving won't cause you to sink. In fact, slow back-and-forth movements can actually let water into the cavity around a trapped limb, loosening the quicksand's hold."* [4]

It is vital that we don't give up hope. I find it interesting that the first step in getting out of quicksand is to stop struggling and lean back. When we lean back into Jesus to allow His healing wisdom and grace flow over us, we can listen to His voice and worship Him. This voluntary movement is like slowly moving back and forth. Leaning into the Lord allows Living Water to flow around the areas of our lives that have been in captivity. As the Living Water begins to surround us, hope is nourished, and forgiveness is received. Even as this is happening, the demonic inroads are being washed away by the Living Water of God. Precious child of God, when we lean into Him, His Living Water brings life to all that is of Him and destroys that which is not of Him.

There are times when our pride, shame and insecurity are the challenges along the path. During these seasons, we are at great risk. Using our quicksand analogy again, "*Getting out will take a while, though. Physicists have calculated that the force required to extract your foot from quicksand at a rate of one centimeter per second is roughly equal to the force needed to lift a medium-sized car.*"[5]

The Psalmist David experienced this when he stated, "*Deeper and deeper I sink into the mire; I can't find a foothold. I am in deep water, and the floods overwhelm me.*"[6] Our impossible problems, hurts, pains, and dysfunctions are not impossible for God. He has more than enough wisdom and strength to pull us free no matter how deeply we are stuck.

> "*So God has given both His promise and His oath. These two things are unchangeable because it is impossible for God to lie. Therefore, we who have fled to Him for refuge can have great confidence as we hold to the hope that lies before us.*"[7]

> Sometimes in order to stand and fight, we have
> to lean back into the Father's arms.

Beloved, do not allow yourself to become immobilized and believe you are not worthy enough to lean into God. *"One genuine danger is that a person who is immobilized in quicksand could be engulfed and drowned by an incoming tide—quicksand often occur in tidal areas..."*[8] If we allow our minds combined with demonic schemes to have the final say, we open the door to potentially drown in life's regrets, pain and misfortune. However, we have a promise that when we lean back into our precious heavenly Father, He will bring a double share of honor, double portion of prosperity, everlasting joy and more! [9]

There is a myth that we can go so far away that God cannot find us; however, remember a myth doesn't mean it is true. Scripture is the foundation from which we determine truth. Not only does God know exactly where we are, He also has equipped us with every tool that we need to get out of the mire. God loves us so much that He will lift us out and steady us as we learn to walk again.

> *"I can never escape from your Spirit! I can never get away from your presence!"* [10]

> *"He stooped down to lift me out of danger from the desolate pit I was in, out of the muddy mess I had fallen into. Now he's lifted me up into a firm, secure place and steadied me while I walk along his ascending path."* [11]

You've leaned into God as you have journeyed through this book. Rejoice in who He is. Rejoice in who He has made you. Celebrate with great and joyful expectation as you look ahead. Allow yourself to dream with God about your future.

As you lean into God, as He pulls you even further toward safety and steadies your feet, you will do more than stand, you will soar.

> *"Have you never heard? Have you never understood? The Lord is the everlasting God, the Creator of all the earth. He never grows weak or wary. No one can measure the depths of His understanding. He gives power to the weak and strength to the powerless. Even youths will become weak and tired, and young men will fall in exhaustion. But those who trust in the Lord will find new strength. They will soar high on the wings like eagles. They will run and not grow weary. They will walk and not faint."* [12]

DECLARATION:

I will not allow my fears, woundings, insecurities or inhibitions to determine my future. I will allow God alone to determine my future. Everything about me is positioned to move forward and to walk into my destiny. Everything within me is clothed with the power of the resurrected Christ. I am an influencer and hold the creative wisdom, insight and ideas that come from the heavenlies. I am a blessing and a child of the King!

Before you close this book – take a moment and ask the Lord what word of encouragement He has for you today and write it below.

_____

_____

_____

———————————————————

———————————————————

———————————————————

———————————————————

———————————————————

———————————————————

———————————————————

———————————————————

———————————————————

———————————————————

———————————————————

———————————————————

———————————————————

———————————————————

———————————————————

NOTE FROM THE AUTHOR

When I was growing up, we spent a week at camp every summer. We sang, and like every camper, I had my favorite songs. Some of those songs became a never-ending loop running through my head for years to come. One of those songs was based on portions of Psalm 18. *"For by You I can crush a troop, and by my God I can leap over a wall."*[1] As we sang the words of that psalm we could see ourselves tearing through troops and leaping over walls to the glory of God. In essence, we all put on our superhero capes and conquered the enemy foe. In addition, Scripture states *"For who is God, but the Lord? Or who is a rock, except our God."²*

Through the years, that song and Scripture began to set a standard that developed into a radical belief in a mighty God, Who alone must be the Rock on which I stand. When we can see from heaven's perspective, we can allow God to position us. We trust that He is faithful to empower and align us to walk into the divine destiny that He has for each and every one of us.

This is a season in which God has invited us to dream with Him. He invites us wholeheartedly into His sphere. He has extended the engraved invitation to see each situation through His lens rather than our own. *"You enlarge the path beneath me and make my steps secure, so that my feet will not slip."³*

He is calling out for us to be free. He encourages us to allow Him to bring healing to all our fears and insecurities, for we were not created to carry them. As our loving heavenly Father, He is looking ahead and encouraging us. I hear Him saying to each one of us "You can do this, just hang onto Me."

He is asking us to trust Him through the traumas of life and to allow Him to plant a garden in the midst of our pain. He is the loving Father who wraps His everlasting love around us and tells our hearts to beat again. He is the One who tenderly encourages us to dare to dream once again.

He invites us into His sphere, a realm where the seemingly impossible becomes possible, a sphere where He heals our wounds and teaches us to see through His lens as He asks the question, *Do you see what I see?* As we learn to *see*, our entire stance changes. We stand up straight as we assume our position as heirs to the Kingdom of Heaven.

Remember, you are of royal blood. You are a son or daughter of the King and He will faithfully position you to walk into the fullness of your divine destiny.

As you have journeyed with me through this book, I hope you have been able to don your Superman/Superwoman cape. When we are running with God, there is no kryptonite because He is the God of the impossible. He has called us to be mighty men and women of God, able to do great exploits for His Kingdom. He invites us to have an impact in our world and to leave a legacy that extends into generations to come.

You may have come to the end of the book, but you are at the beginning of the next leg of your journey. Dream with God; run your race; make an impact; and fall deeper and deeper in love with the lover of your soul. So, run through the troops and over the walls and shout hallelujah! Allow Him to become the Rock on which you stand. Enjoy the journey and you'll be amazed at the places you will go and the things you will see as you journey with the King of Kings and Lord of Lords.

ABOUT THE AUTHOR

Ruth Hendrickson is a conference speaker, ministry trainer, and board-certified biblical counselor with extensive experience in the development, training, and oversight of emotional healing ministry teams, recovery ministries, prophetic ministry, prayer ministries and women's ministry. Most recently, she served for more than thirteen years on the pastoral staff of a Spirit-filled United Methodist Church. In addition, she is a course facilitator for Patricia King Institute and an ordained minister with the American Presbyterian Church.

Ruth is passionate about training, equipping, and releasing individuals to walk in freedom and wholeness through both physical and emotional healing. Through biblically-based teachings and practical applications infused with love and laughter, her goal is to introduce people not only to the living God Who saves, but also to the God Who desires an intimate relationship with each one of His children.

Ruth is an avid unsweetened ice tea drinker who loves warm weather, palm trees and beaches! Needless to say, she believes that she should live in the South. However, in the meantime Ruth and her husband Mark reside in Stockton, New Jersey and have five adult children.

www.RuthHendrickson.org

INVITE RUTH TO SPEAK AT YOUR NEXT EVENT

To check her availability, email
info@ruthhendrickson.org

ENDNOTES

CHAPTER 1

1. www.goodreads.com/author/quotes/43395.Bill_Johnson Accessed 6/5/18. Bill Johnson, Spiritual Java.

2. See Matthew 18:3

3. Psalm 139:13-16 TPT

4. www.bradley.edu/sites/bodyproject/male-body-image-m-vs-f. Accessed 9/7/18

5. 1 Corinthians 13:12 NLT

6. Matthew 7:4 TPT

7. 1 Corinthians 14:33 NLT

8. Ephesians 1:17-18 NLT

9. Coekin, Richard. *Ephesians For You.* The Good Book Company, 2015, p35.

10. Ephesians 1:18 NLT

11. Acts 7:54-60 NLT

12. Acts 9:1-9 NLT

13. Acts 9:17-18 NLT

14. Philippians 3:5-6 NLT

15. Philippians 3:13-14 NLT

16. Wikipedia contributors. "Me generation." *Wikipedia, The Free Encyclopedia.* Wikipedia, The Free Encyclopedia, 7 Apr. 2018. Web. 21 Apr. 2018. Accessed 4/21/18. https://en.wikipedia.org/wiki/Me_generation

CHAPTER 2

1. https://quotesss.com/author/21147-heidi-bakerAccessed 9/21/18

2. "Identity" *Websters 1828 Dictionary* http://webstersdictionary1828.com/Dictionary/belief. Accessed 4/21/18

3. "Change in Terminology: "Mental Retardation" to "Intellectual Disability." *Federal Register The Daily Journal of the United States Government,* 8/1/2013. Accessed 4/21/18.

4. See 1 Samuel 16

5. See Genesis 1:27

6. Jeremiah 1:5 NLT

7. Psalm 18:29 NLT

8. 1 Samuel 17:26 NLT

9. 1 Samuel 17:32-37 NLT

10. "How Tall Was Goliath." GotQuestions.org, www.gotquestions.org/how-tall-was-Goliath.html. Accessed 4/22/18

11. Cornwall, Judson Dr., Smith, Stelman, Dr. *The Exhaustive Dictionary of Bible Names.* Bridge-Logos, 1998, p. 43.

12. Cornwall, Judson Dr., Smith, Stelman, Dr. *The Exhaustive Dictionary of Bible Names.* Bridge-Logos, 1998, p. 61.

13. 1 Samuel 17:38-39 NLT

14. Proverbs 3:5-6 AMP

15. 1 Samuel 17:40 NLT

16. 1 Samuel 13:14 NLT

CHAPTER 3

1. www.allchristianquotes.org/authors/472/Che_Ahn/. Accessed 9/21/18.

2. "Label" *Websters 1828 Dictionary.* http://webstersdictionary1828. com/Dictionary/label Accessed 4/24/18.

3. I Am Covered Over. www.higherpraise.com/lyrics/elder/ elder_0068.html. Accessed 09/19/18.

4. Judges 6:2 NLT

5. Judges 6:11 NLT

6. Psalm 139:7 NLT

7. Judges 6:12 NLT

8. Judges 6:12 NLT

9. Judges 6:14 NLT

10. Judges 6:15 NLT

11. Judges 6:25-31 NLT

12. Judges 6:33-40 NLT

13. Judges 7:3 NLT

14. Judges 7:9-14 NLT

15. Matthew 16:16 AMP

16. Matthew 16:17-19 AMP

17. Matthew 16:22-23 AMP

18. Jeremiah 29:11 NLT

19. Matthew 16:16 NLT

20. Cornwall, Dr. Judson, Smith, Dr. Stelman. *The Exhaustive Dictionary of Bible Names.* Alachua. Bridge-Logos 1998, p. 89.

21. "Mire." *Merriam-Webster.com.* Merriam-Webster, n.d. Web. 25 Apr. 2018.

22. 1 Chronicles 4:9-10 NLT

23. Cooper, Charles. *A Look at the Prayer of Jabez.* Grace Sola Foundation, Inc. www.solagroup.org/articles/christianliving/cl_0004.html. Accessed 10/16/17.

24. See Galatians 3:13

CHAPTER 4

1. www.brainyquote.com/quotes/john_wesley_524891. Accessed 6/8/18

2. "Fear" Websters 1828 Dictionary. http://webstersdictionary1828.com/Dictionary/fear. Accessed 4/26/18

3. "Insecurity" Websters 1828 Dictionary. http://webstersdictionary1828.com/Dictionary/insecurity. Accessed 4/26/18

4. "Kissing Cousin." Merriam-Webster.com. Merriam-Webster, n.d. Web. 26 Apr. 2018.

5. Isaiah 40:31 AMP

6. 1 Kings 18:17 NLT

7. 1 Kings 18:38-39 NLT

8. 1 Kings 18:45 NLT

9. 1 Kings 19:1-3 NLT

10. See 1 Kings 19:1-9 NLT

11. Packer, J.I. Knowing God. Hodder & Stoughton, 1975 quoted in Coekin, Richard. Ephesians for You. The Good Book Company. 2015. p. 33-34.

12. See Hebrews 13:5

13. 2 Kings 19:11-13 NLT

14. See 2 Kings 18:18

15. Ecclesiastes 4:9-10 NLT

16. Psalm 5:11 TPT

17. Nadia. 5 Benefits of Building Blocks. Fun with Mama. www.funwithmama.com/812/. Accessed 4/27/18

18. See Revelation 21:5

19. See Nehemiah 1:11

20. Nehemiah 2:2 NLT

21. Nehemiah 2:2 NLT

22. Nehemiah 2:4-5 NLT

23. See Nehemiah 1:3-11

24. Nehemiah 2:1-9 NLT

25. 1 Peter 5:8 TPT

26. Nehemiah 2:19 NLT

27. See Nehemiah 4:15-22

28. Luke 6:47-48 TPT

CHAPTER 5

1. www.goodreads.com/author/quotes/95474.R_T_
Kendall?page=2. Accessed 9/25/18

2. "Unforgiven" http://webstersdictionary1828.com/Dictionary/
Unforgiven. Accessed 4/29/18

3. "Forgiveness" http://webstersdictionary1828.com/Dictionary/
forgiveness. Accessed 4/29/18

4. Ahn, Che. Look up, God is With You. The Elijah List. April 29,
2018. Accessed 4/29/18. http://elijahlist.com/words/display_
word.html?ID=20065

5. Acts 7:60 TPT

6. Zavada, Jack. "Stoning of Stephen - Bible Story Summary." ThoughtCo, Aug. 15, 2016, thoughtco.com/stoning-of-stephen-bible-story-summary-700061. Accessed April 30, 2018

7. Proverbs 27:6 AMP

8. See Psalm 18:30; 145:17, Deuteronomy 32:4

9. Matthew 18:21 NLT

10. Matthew 18:22 NLT

11. Historical information gleaned from: "What did Jesus mean when He said that we should forgive others seventy times seven? God Questions. www.gotquestions.org/seventy-times-seven.html. Accessed 5/1/18

12. Ephesians 4:32 TPT

13. Accessed 6/8/18.

14. Jeremiah 29: 11-14 NLT

CHAPTER 6

1. www.tdjakes.com/posts/5-t-d-jakes-quotes-that-remind-us-to-never-give-up. Accessed 9/21/18.

2. "Trauma." *Merriam-Webster.com*. Merriam-Webster, n.d. Web. 6 May 2018.

3. Esther 2:2 NLT

4. Esther 2:2, 8 NLT

5. Genesis 4:2-7 NLT

6. www.biblestudytools.com/commentaries/wesleys-explanatory-notes/genesis/genesis-4.html. Accessed 5-6-18.

7. Genesis 4:7 NLT

8. Genesis 4:7 NLT

9. See the Book of Job

10. See Job 3, Job 6,

11. Job 6:10 NLT

12. Job 42:5-6 NLT

13. Job 42:12 NLT

14. See Proverbs 2:10, Luke 21:15, James 1:5

15. See Matthew 27:51

16. See Hebrews 4:14-16

17. 2 Corinthians 1:3-11 NLT

CHAPTER 7

1. www.facebook.com/evangelistreinhardbonnke/photos/a.1015041 7025670258/10155488539210258/?type=1&theater. Accessed 9/21/18.

2. Basis for declaration is 1 John 4:4

3. Job 1:6-12 NLT

4. Luke 22:31-32 TPT

5. 1 Peter 5:8 NLT

6. Job 2:2 NLT

7. 1 Peter 5:9 NLT

8. See Genesis 18:16-23

9. Genesis 18:24 NLT

10. Genesis 19:17-20 NLT

11. Genesis 19:23-26 NLT

12. Job 42:12-16 NLT

13. Cornwall, Judson Dr., Smith, Stelman, Dr. *The Exhaustive Dictionary of Bible Names*. Alachua. Bridge-Logos. 1998, p. 105.

14. Cornwall, Judson Dr., Smith, Stelman, Dr. *The Exhaustive Dictionary of Bible Names*. Alachua. Bridge-Logos. 1998, p. 96.

15. Cornwall, Judson Dr., Smith, Stelman, Dr. *The Exhaustive Dictionary of Bible Names*. Alachua. Bridge-Logos. 1998, p. 117.

16. Cornwall, Judson Dr., Smith, Stelman, Dr. *The Exhaustive Dictionary of Bible Names*. Alachua. Bridge-Logos. 1998, p. 115.

17. Ephesians 6:10-13 AMP

18. 2 Corinthians 10:5 NLT

19. Hebrews 12:3 TPT

20. Matthew 4:1-11 NLT

21. Hebrews 2:17-18 TPT

22. 1 Corinthians 10:13 TPT

CHAPTER 8

1. www.allchristianquotes.org/authors/22/Smith_
   Wigglesworth/65-80/. Accessed 9/21/18.

2. Proverbs 3:5-6 TPT

3. Hebrews 4:12 TPT

4. "Kairos." *Merriam-Webster.com*. Merriam-Webster, n.d. Web. 19
   May 2018.

5. Luke 1:38 TPT

6. Isaiah 54:11 NLT

7. Exodus 14:13-14 NLT

8. Isaiah 52:12 NLT

9. Exodus 14:15-16 NLT

10. Matthew 17:20 TPT

11. 2 Samuel 23:8 NLT

12. Cornwall, Judson Dr., Smith, Stelman, Dr. *The Exhaustive
    Dictionary of Bible Names*. Alachua. Bridge-Logos. 1998, p.92.

13. Cornwall, Judson Dr., Smith, Stelman, Dr. *The Exhaustive
    Dictionary of Bible Names*. Alachua. Bridge-Logos. 1998, p. 65

14. 2 Samuel 23:9-10 NLT

15. See Matthew 4 when Satan tried to tempt Jesus

16. Cornwall, Judson Dr., Smith, Stelman, Dr. *The Exhaustive
    Dictionary of Bible Names*. Alachua. Bridge-Logos. 1998, p. 47.

17. Cornwall, Judson Dr., Smith, Stelman, Dr. *The Exhaustive Dictionary of Bible Names*. Alachua. Bridge-Logos. 1998, p. 45.

18. Cornwall, Judson Dr., Smith, Stelman, Dr. *The Exhaustive Dictionary of Bible Names*. Alachua. Bridge-Logos. 1998, p. 9.

19. 2 Corinthians 10:3-4 TPT

20. Ephesians 6:11 NLT

21. 2 Samuel 23:11-12 NLT

22. Cornwall, Judson Dr., Smith, Stelman, Dr. *The Exhaustive Dictionary of Bible Names*. Alachua. Bridge-Logos. 1998, p. 166

23. Philippians 3:13-14 TPT

24. Isaiah 54:11 NLT

CONCLUSION

1. www.goodreads.com/author/quotes/167703.Kris_Vallotton. Accessed 6/8/18.

2. www.britannica.com/story/how-deadly-is-quicksand. Accessed 5/20/18

3. Luke 1:37 TPT

4. www.britannica.com/story/how-deadly-is-quicksand. Accessed 5/20/18

5. www.britannica.com/story/how-deadly-is-quicksand. Accessed 5/20/18

6. Psalm 69:2 NLT

7. Hebrews 6:18 NLT

8. www.britannica.com/story/how-deadly-is-quicksand. Accessed 5/20/18

9. See Isaiah 61:7

10. Psalm 139:7 NLT

11. Psalm 40:2 TPT

12. Isaiah 40:28-31 NLT

NOTE FROM THE AUTHOR

1. Psalm 18:29 AMP

2. Psalm 18:31 AMP

3. Psalm 18:36 AMP

BIBLES CITED

WORKS CITED

Ahn, Che. *Look up, God is With You.* The Elijah List. April 29, 2018. http://elijahlist.com/words/display_word.html?ID=20065

www.allchristianquotes.org/authors/22/Smith_ Wigglesworth/65-80/.

www.biblestudytools.com/commentaries/wesleys-explanatory-notes/ genesis/genesis-4.html.

www.facebook.com/evangelistreinhardbonnke/photos/a.101504170 25670258/10155488539210258/?type=1&theater.

www.bradley.edu/sites/bodyproject/male-body-image-m-vs-f/.

www.brainyquote.com/quotes/john_wesley_524891.

www.britannica.com/story/how-deadly-is-quicksand.

www.christianquotes.info/quotes-by-topic/quotes-about-forgiveness /?listpage=4&instance=2#participants-list-2.

Coekin, Richard. *Ephesians For You.* The Good Book Company, 2015

Cooper, Charles. *A Look at the Prayer of Jabez.* Grace Sola Foundation, Inc. www.solagroup.org/articles/christianliving/ cl_0004.html.

Cornwall, Judson Dr., Smith, Stelman, Dr. *The Exhaustive Dictionary of Bible Names.* Bridge-Logos, 1998

"Change in Terminology: "Mental Retardation" to "Intellectual Disability." *Federal Register The Daily Journal of the United States Government*, 8/1/2013.

I Am Covered Over. http://www.higherpraise.com/lyrics/elder/ elder_0068.html. Accessed 09/19/18.

"How Tall Was Goliath." GotQuestions.org, https://www. gotquestions.org/how-tall-was-Goliath.html.

www.goodreads.com/author/quotes/43395.Bill_Johnson, Spiritual Java.

Historical information gleaned from: "What did Jesus mean when He said that we should forgive others seventy times seven? God Questions. www.gotquestions.org/seventy-times-seven.html.

Merriam-Webster.com. Merriam-Webster, n.d. Web.

Nadia. 5 Benefits of Building Blocks. Fun with Mama. www. funwithmama.com/812/.

Packer, J.I. *Knowing God.* Hodder & Stoughton, 1975 quoted in Coekin, Richard. *Ephesians for You.* The Good Book Company. 2015.

https://quotesss.com/author/21147-heidi-baker

www.tdjakes.com/posts/5-t-d-jakes-quotes-that-remind-us-to-never-give-up.

Websters 1828 Dictionary http://webstersdictionary1828.com/ Dictionary/belief.

Wikipedia contributors. "Me Generation." *Wikipedia, The*